To Stephanie, who inspired this book in the
first place, and to women everywhere.

URBAN REVOLUTIONS

A Woman's Guide to Two-Wheeled Transportation

All text is © Emilie Bahr
This edition is © by Microcosm Publishing, 2016
Cover design and layout/illustrations by Meggyn Pomerleau
The typefaces used in this book are Baskerville & Bella Pro
The illustration on this page was done by Elaine Guillot
Photo credits are as they appear on page 189.

First Printing, May 10, 2016

For a catalog, write
Microcosm Publishing
2752 N. Williams Ave
Portland, OR 97227
or visit MicrocosmPublishing.com

ISBN 978-1-62106-912-6
This is Microcosm #196

Distributed worldwide by Legato /
Perseus and in the UK by Turnaround
This book was printed on post-
consumer paper in the United States.

Library of Congress Cataloging-in-
Publication Data

Names: Bahr, Emilie, author.
Title: Urban revolutions : a woman's guide to two-wheeled transportation / by
    Emilie Bahr.
Description: Portland, Oregon : Microcosm Pub., [2016]
Identifiers: LCCN 2015035135 | ISBN 9781621069126
Subjects: LCSH: Cycling for women—United States. | Cycling—United States. |
    Bicycle commuting—United States.
Classification: LCC GV1057 .B35 2016 | DDC 796.6082—dc23
LC record available at http://lccn.loc.gov/2015035135

Microcosm Publishing .com

N WILLIAMS AVE. • PORTLAND, OR 97227 • 2752

GROW YOUR SMALL WORLD • MADE IN THE USA

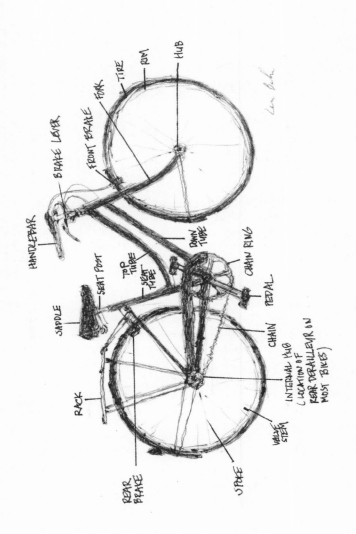

HUB

RIM

TIRE

FORK

FRONT BRAKE

BRAKE LEVER

HANDLEBAR

DOWN TUBE

CHAIN RING

PEDAL

SEAT POST

TOP TUBE

SEAT TUBE

SADDLE

CHAIN

INTERNAL HUB
(LOCATION OF
REAR DERAILLEUR ON
MOST BIKES)

RACK

VALVE STEM

REAR BRAKE

SPOKE

TABLE OF

CONTENTS

There was a time not very long ago when it never would have

occurred to me to hop on my bike to travel from point A to point B. I knew that biking was healthy and environmentally-friendly. I also had a vague recognition that in certain parts of the world, the bike was an essential mode of transportation, unlike the hunk of metal collecting rust and cobwebs in my mother's shed. My brother had even sold his car years earlier and gotten around exclusively by bike and transit. But he lived in Chicago while I lived in New Orleans, which, I long assumed, somehow gave me a pass.

My city is known for its culinary traditions, bars that never close, and the strong likelihood that at any given time, music is erupting spontaneously in the street. Given our legendary focus on letting the good times roll, it's perhaps unsurprising that we haven't always worried much about health and fitness, the environment, the latest in infrastructure trends, or generally about what people in the rest of the world are doing. This is a place, after all, where the mantra "so far behind we're ahead" is worn as a badge of pride.

Back in 2007, when I was working as a reporter at a local magazine, I decided to write about a seemingly anomalous plan to install new bike lanes on roads set for reconstruction post Hurricane Katrina. They would be the first on-street bike facilities in the city. Seeking to illustrate the city's utter inhospitality to cyclists, I went in search of a bicycle commuter. As I didn't yet know any members of this exotic tribe, I enlisted the help of a representative of the local bike-advocacy group to aid in my quest. Where I had anticipated a disheveled, daredevil adrenaline junkie, the bike commuter I interviewed was a neat, soft-spoken, middle-aged man employed by a local university. Instead of regaling me with harrowing tales, his description of pedaling across town to get between home and work made the act seem at once exciting and romantic, and also remarkably … ordinary.

It's hard to understate how much has changed since that fateful interview where biking is concerned. A confluence of factors has helped to swell New Orleans' bicycling ranks to the point where we are now positioned among the top large cities in the U.S. for the rate of people commuting by bike. Where it was once viewed as a means of last resort, bicycling is increasingly seen as a practical and, dare I say it, fashionable mode of transportation here, and in a growing number of cities across the country and around the globe.

My own perspective has changed just as dramatically as my city's landscape. Not long after I wrote the story about the city's new investment in bicycling, I quit my magazine job and enrolled in urban planning school. On the first day of class, I couldn't stop smiling as my classmates introduced themselves by giving their names and the routes they used to bike to school. I took pride in the fact that my commute was one of the longest.

It was in school that I was first introduced to a troubling statistic related to women and bicycling. As is the case with wages, potential for career advancement, and, generally speaking, the ability to detect dirt splattered on the kitchen floor, there is a stubborn gap between the sexes when it comes to willingness to ride a bike. According to Census estimates, only about a quarter of American bike commuters are female. Yet, as I would discover when I delved deeper into the topic, these statistics don't adequately reflect the strong—and I would argue growing—interest among many women in getting around by bike.

There are a variety of explanations put forth to explain the biking gender gap, from the male-centric marketing strategies of bicycle manufacturers to a higher risk-aversion among women to gender norms and social policies that continue to place the bulk of child-rearing and household responsibilities on women. Biking alone is one thing; carting around a child and groceries is another.

While I'm certain each of these factors plays a role, I think another set of cultural forces exerts significant sway. After all, the disparity between the sexes is not universal. In the Netherlands and Denmark, which boast some of the highest levels of bicycling in the developed world, women are in the cycling majority. The same is true in certain New Orleans neighborhoods, based on the best estimates available, and perhaps in certain parts of your own town.

In the presence of plentiful role models, women, like other groups, appear to more readily embrace bicycling as viable, safe, and socially acceptable. To me, this represents an exciting opportunity. It means that those of us who ride our bikes might think of ourselves as cycling ambassadors. As we're out bicycling the streets, we can help to encourage other women to consider the possibility.

I should probably mention here that I do not ride my bike every day. As much as I would like to claim my only modes of transportation as my bike and the streetcar that runs a block away from my house, there are times when life, my legs, the weather, and the

The American Community Survey, which is sent out to a random sample of city residents every year, asks participants how they got to work most often in the previous week. I have yet to be surveyed by the Census Bureau about how I get to work, but if the opportunity ever arises, I very badly want to be able to claim my bike as my primary commute mode.

convenience of the car parked outside my apartment get in the way.

During the workweek, I'm pretty happy with myself if I make it to the office on my bike three out of the five days I go in.

This rather arbitrary goal is inspired by the standards set by the U.S. Census Bureau to determine one's commute mode.

This is all to say that in order to become a bicyclist, you don't have to sell your car, move across town to be closer to your job, and throw yourself into alternative-transportation activism. But be forewarned, these are all not-infrequent side effects of developing a bicycling habit.

This book, designed to be toted around for quick reference, aims to help break through some of the barriers women face in opting to get on their bikes, especially in the car-dependent southern U.S. where I live and in other locales where there aren't always great roads or role models encouraging the practice. It draws on academic research, trial and error, and the tips I've picked up from fellow cyclists (female and male) along the way. I hope it offers you the inspiration and confidence to get on your bike, and that this experience changes your life in as many positive ways as it has mine.

My Life,
By Bike

My Life By Bike

The first bike I ever remember riding is the almost-antique Trek now lodged in the back of my mom's overcrowded shed, its once shiny black varnish dulled with the patina of its close-to-four-decade existence. My mom used that bike to transport me around town starting when I was six months old, back when she and my dad were still married and he taught at the university where she was a student at the time. We bopped around town together on that bike, my head bobbing behind her beneath the weight of the large, round crate of an adult helmet stuffed with balled up newspapers, my body propped up in the child seat with pillows. I'm quite certain none of this was pediatrician-approved, but we didn't have much money back then, nor were safety standards of the day exactly so exacting, and in any case, they may not have made anything else more child-appropriate.

I am in my new neighborhood with my friend Ashley. We have recently moved from our old Victorian home without air conditioning in a poor part of town near the university, where Mom made friends by doling out vegetables from her organic garden and where my brother was mugged before he turned ten. (The thieves made off with his bike, it being the only thing he had of value.) It was also where a nine-month-old me crawled out of the screen door and across the street to visit the neighbor's dog, only to be readily identified as the only toe-headed baby on the block, and swiftly returned home to my embarrassed mother, who had been sleeping soundly in a child-rearing/breast-feeding-induced coma on the couch.

We have moved, for reasons not apparent to me, to a new subdivision across town with neat, manicured yards and tidy homes and where the only people of color are the neighbors across the street who bake themselves the color of burnt sweet potatoes every summer, roasting in their front yards, their skin slick with baby oil.

Mom has taken a corporate job, trading her flowing festival skirts and anti-war T-shirts for shoulder-padded suits, lots of hairspray, and red lipstick. Her bike, too, has been relinquished in favor of the boat-like company car that she uses to travel across the state peddling medical supplies. Whereas at our old home she spent hours playing with me in the yard, teaching me how to tell when the peas and tomatoes were ripe enough to pick, now she spends most of her time when she's not driving around babbling into the phone in her new lexicon dominated by such phrases as "in-servicing" and "touching base." Dad by this time has lost his university job and taken to long-distance running as his occupation of choice.

Our new neighborhood has few distinguishing characteristics, excepting the steep hill at its entrance off the main road. I am about five and have just gotten the training wheels off of my bike, giddy and terrified by testing the boundaries of my newly acquired skill. Ashley is a couple years older and has had her training wheels removed for some time, and as we stand at the top of the hill looking out over cul-de-sacs and tract homes, Ashley insists (and I do not resist) that we switch bikes.

I start my descent from what might as well be Kilimanjaro, gliding without any effort at all and picking up speed until I am flying through the wind in a way I have never flown before. I know before it happens what will come next as my feet slip off the out-of-control pedals and in slow motion my head starts to tumble toward the pavement in an ill-timed summersault. When I arrive home, the shriek and look on my mother's face cause the tears and pain to expand three-fold. I have two teeth missing and another pushed back toward my tonsils that I can't stop jabbing with my tongue. Fortunately, they are only baby teeth.

I am eleven. My parents have divorced and I'm living with my single dad in what was once proudly touted as our city's first subdivision, constructed in the 1940s for doctors and lawyers and the rest of the upper crust and so thoroughly modern at the time that its originators saw no need to install sidewalks, this being a place built for the rapidly-growing contingent of car owners. Now the neighborhood is starting its inexorable transition to a place of middle-class plant workers and other families of modest means, the others having died off or moved deeper into suburbia or back to the parts of town where you can actually walk to get places. Dad has moved us here so he can be close to his job and so that I can be just down the street from my best friend, Erin.

It is somewhat ironic that in this GM paradise I come to recognize, suddenly and without warning, the urgent need for a bike. Despite years of abstinence, the allure of bike ownership has become so overpowering that I take to recounting it multiple times a day to my ever-patient father. He listens intently to my pitch then says simply, "We'll see." This providing more than ample fuel for my fantasizing,

I take to imagining my vastly-improved life with my new bike in possession, traveling the distance to Erin's house in record speed, the feeling of the wind whipping my hair, the unprecedented freedom I will experience in its saddle, even if that freedom stops at the periphery of our subdivision of tree-lined boulevards and mid-century homes hemmed in by highways.

A bike becomes the currency by which all else is measured, the only thing, I tell my father, I will ever need in life to be happy. (Later, this will also be the case with the Nintendo gaming system and, later still, a pair of Girbaud jeans.) Because I have a parent who, despite his meager income, is both highly susceptible to the whims of his demanding daughter and obsessed with physical fitness, he can find no reason to deny me. It isn't long before Dad comes home with a cobalt blue mountain bike with silver trim, and I ride circles around and around the neighborhood, returning at nightfall exhausted. After some time, as is often the case with the things we most desire, the novelty wears off and my bike is spending most of the time propped against a wall in the laundry room. Eventually, someone comes in the middle of the day while Dad and I are away and takes my bike, positioned in very plain view through the window of the unlocked laundry room door. I will never see that bike again. Dad tries to console me, explaining that the person who took the bike was obviously desperate, probably needed it to get to a job to support his own little girl. But really, I'm not very worried, my bike fascination having already started to give way to other concerns, such as New Kids on the Block, spying on Erin's older brother, and inventing new dance moves.

Eleven years later, I am standing with my boyfriend in a bike shop in Washington, D.C. I don't own a car, but transportation is not what has brought me into this shop, what with the subway system so reliable and my boyfriend's car keys so readily available. Rather, I am again feeling an urge to take to the saddle, this time after hearing of the mountain biking opportunities to be found in the nearby Virginia hills. The bike I will select that day is chosen with this activity in mind, and because it is one of the cheapest in the store, and because its blue matches that of the mountain bike stolen from the laundry room so many years before. Within the hour, I will have a change of heart and bring it back to the store, thankful they allow me to exchange it for the red one, which I have determined looks more serious, more rugged, more like that of a Real Bicyclist.

I mountain bike exactly once on that bike and for the rest of my days in D.C. it will occupy an inordinate amount of real estate in the basement apartment I share with a college friend. It will soon be tossed into the back of the moving truck that transports my boyfriend and me back south to New Orleans. Shortly thereafter, I will drag it with me to the small Cajun town where I have been hired for my first real job writing for the local newspaper. In three years there, my bike will be ridden one time, for an ill-conceived, 75-mile bike ride in the heat of July to coincide with the Tour de France along the gravel-strewn, eighteen-wheeler-heavy highway that hugs Bayou Lafourche. I convince my boss to let me take this trip and write about it, and he agrees, if reluctantly, and I ask my co-worker to come with me. At the end of the ride, my conservative Christian editor arrives to pick us up and the first words out of his mouth upon surveying our sunburned, withered bodies in our shorts and tank tops are: "Next time, we'll have to discuss a more appropriate wardrobe, ladies." I feel the distinct urge to punch him in the face, but my body is so stiff with fatigue and my hands so numb from gripping the handlebars that fortunately, I refrain.

Instead, I move back to New Orleans, where my bike winds up pushed to the back of my mother's compact shed, behind gardening equipment, paint, stackable chairs, and related ephemera, and somewhat poetically, I'd say, next to her old Trek. It is upon my return to the city following a short-lived exile after Hurricane Gustav (Katrina's thankfully benign cousin) in 2008 that I head to my mom's house, squeezing past the thorns of a toppled bougainvillea that is blocking the shed, to pull that bike out again, figuring it is the best mechanism for surveying the debris-strewn streets. Shortly thereafter, I take to riding it to festivals, where the throngs of people and the inability to park even remotely close by makes biking the obvious option, even if it has taken me some time to notice. I suggest to a boyfriend in from out of town that we travel downtown to the Fat Tuesday festivities by bike and when he balks, we take an overcrowded bus instead. We break up shortly thereafter.

I am biking home from Jazz Fest on an otherwise tranquil evening in April of the following year with yet another boyfriend when three kids emerge out of the darkness and in an instant surround us, pointing guns at our faces. I fall off of my bike as the kids demand our cash, which we promptly turn over, and sit bleeding on the curb as they rifle through my boyfriend's billfold. "Can I have my bike back?" I ask bizarrely, in a surge of near-death-induced bravado. "We don't want your bike," the tiniest of them manages before the trio runs away into the night. The scar that forms on my right arm where the flesh is scraped away in that incident looks as though it were created by an eagle's talons, and I wear it proudly as a tattoo for several years until it mostly fades away.

Three years later, I have a new soon-to-be-boyfriend. He and I, I discover in the short time we have known one another, have an uncanny amount in common. A love of music, dancing, and *A Confederacy of Dunces*. A passion for the coast. Our mothers come from the same small town. I know there has to be a deal-breaker in there somewhere, so I try not to get my hopes up but do anyway. "He's probably a Republican," I think to myself. One night, we are in the midst of a very long phone call when I share with him what is by now one of my defining characteristics. "I'm really into biking," I say, then adding, to clarify that I don't mean in the recreational, sporty sense, but that my biking affinity is more along the lines of the all-encompassing-as-to-border-on-the-obsessive variety, "For transportation." I wait for a sigh or some other dismissive signal. "So am I," he tells me. "Uh oh," we both remember thinking.

Just before Christmas the following year, he will present me with the most beautiful bicycle I have ever owned. It is a sleek, steel-gray city bike with matching brown leather handlebars and saddle. It comes with panniers that attach easily and elegantly to the rear rack, thus eliminating the heavy backpack that has become a source of nagging neck pain on my long commutes to work and school. It even has fenders that will ward off the Jackson Pollack effect that once developed on my back every time I rode after a rainstorm. It is a perfect gift from my near-perfect boyfriend, even if it brings with it a new set of challenges.

I learn to pitch my body in just the right way to lug it up my stairs. I worry about it getting scratched when I lock it up outside. I border on hysteria as I stand, stranded, waiting for someone to arrive to help me for the third time in as many weeks after I hear the telltale hissing of yet another flat. My mountain bike, I think, never got flats. I start to wonder if I have made the wrong decision about trading in my bike but also, in especially frustrating moments, in my choice of mates. I worry that perhaps like this seemingly perfect bike, this man isn't so perfect for me after all. But shortly thereafter, I will learn to fix a flat, along with a few other key maintenance maneuvers, and that my original problem had been the result of some poorly applied rim tape. I also come to recognize that bikes, like relationships, take patience, love, and a good bit of elbow grease.

And so, it is this man who, exactly four months ago as I write this, I married and rode off into the night with, me in my white wedding dress hiked up around my knees on a borrowed vintage cruiser; him in his handsome grey suit on the red road bike that we share between us and affectionately call (in the way that some might call a puppy) Allez. Our closest friends and family members crowded around us, cheering as we rolled off into the distance on a warm September night, our bike lights flashing in the fog.

"I stand and rejoice every time I see a woman ride by on a wheel...the picture of free, untrammeled womanhood."
-Susan B. Anthony [1]

Pedaling Toward Equity

As I write this, there are signs that the only country remaining in the world where women are expressly prohibited from getting behind the wheel may soon ease its ban on women driving.[2]

A Saudi Arabian advisory council has suggested to the country's leadership that certain women be allowed to drive themselves around, provided they are at least 30 years old, are not wearing makeup, drive during daylight hours, and have been granted permission by a male guardian.[3] This follows on the heels of a surging resistance to the ban by gutsy Saudi Arabian women who have staged dramatic acts of civil disobedience simply by getting into the driver's seat and posting their flagrant disregard for the law, in the way of every modern protest movement, to YouTube and other social media outlets.[4]

Thinking about the driving ban got me wondering about how else women in this notoriously oppressive society might be getting around. Because it is a country that is quite literally built upon abundant, cheap oil, public transportation isn't much of an option. Could it be then, I wondered, that Saudi Arabia was abuzz with women bicyclists? The answer, I quickly discovered, is a resounding no. It turns out the same conservative leaders who have barred women from obtaining drivers licenses have effectively banned women from bicycling too. As a result, women who want to legally move around their country are reliant almost exclusively on the willingness of a man to drive them around. Because women of means can afford to hire a driver, the restrictions on mobility most seriously affect the poor.

The ban on women bicyclists isn't unique to Saudi Arabia. Fundamentalists in North Korea and Iran have also imposed gender-specific restrictions on bicycling. ("It is not a sin for a woman to sit on a bicycle," Iranian Ayatollah Elm Alhuda purportedly reasoned, "provided she does so indoors or in her backyard."[5]) In Egypt, as across much of the Arab world, social norms hold that bicycling is unwomanly.[6] In Afghanistan, sports in general are taboo for women and bicycling is discouraged perhaps above all, based on the belief that the bicycle seat risks deflowering virginal young women. Simply for riding a bike, an Afghani woman faces death threats or worse.[7]

The arguments used today to justify prohibitions on women bicyclists sound remarkably similar to those put forth in this country in the late 19th century, when the arrival of the "safety bicycle" was prompting women and men to take to two wheels in record numbers.[8] A San Francisco newspaper columnist proffered in 1895: "What the interested public wishes to know is, Where are all the women on wheels going? Is there a grand rendezvous somewhere toward which they are all headed and where they will some time hold a meet that will cause this wobbly old world to wake up and readjust itself?"[9] The practice was met with condemnation from some, who predicted giving women access to the bike would result in an unraveling of the very structure upon which society depended.

The conservatives were right to be worried. The bike would prove a game changer, helping to fuel revolutions in spheres from women's fashion to civil rights.[10] It encouraged women to cast off restrictive Victorian corsets and long, heavy skirts that made bicycling difficult in favor of loose-fit bloomers and other selections more conducive to physical activity. Even more importantly, it afforded unprecedented mobility that made it possible for women to get educated, get a job, and be exposed to radical ideas and political organizing as the women's suffrage movement gathered steam.

"I am not an advocate of the use of the bicycle among women," a Chicago police captain named Luke Colleran told the *New York Times* in 1899, according to the rather hilariously-headlined article: "MORALS OF WHEELWOMEN; A Chicago Police Captain Thinks the Use of the Bicycle Dangerous—Mrs. Henrotin Disputes Him."[11]

جولة شامية 2014/12/13

The policeman continued:

> Women of refinement and exquisite moral training
> addicted to the use of the bicycle are not infrequently
> thrown among the uncultivated and degenerate
> elements of both sexes, whose course, boisterous and
> immoral gestures are heard and seen while speeding
> along our streets and boulevards. [Moreover], a
> large number of our female bicyclists wear shorter
> dresses than the laws of morality and decency
> permit, thereby inviting the improper conversations
> and remarks of the depraved and immoral. I most
> certainly consider the adoption of the bicycle by
> women as detrimental to the advancement of
> morality…

Just as the bike stands in some places in the world today as an example of women's oppression, it is also being appropriated as an agent of insurrection among some working to advance women's rights.

A group called Girls Revolution in Egypt encourages women to ignore custom and take to the bike as a way to promote broader social change.[12] Palestinian journalist Asmaa al-Ghul, a secularist and feminist living in Gaza City, has used bicycle riding, among other tools, to protest the Hamas-controlled government and its restrictive treatment of women.[13] The group Yalla Let's Bike formed in 2014 in Damascus, Syria to encourage residents of that country to take to the bike for transportation amid mounting economic stress, skyrocketing fuel prices, and crippling traffic congestion that are the yields of that country's civil war.[14] [15] Although its work aims to foster economic empowerment and environmental stewardship for the benefit of all Syrians, the group's work has as a key part of its agenda promoting gender equality in Syria. "We want to change the norms and social snobbery according to which bicycles are for the poor or male athletes," Sarah al Zein, a student of French literature and one of the organizers of Yalla Let's Bike, told me.[16] Even in Afghanistan, where girls are subjected to acid attacks and other brutalities simply for trying to go to school, a group of valiant women has formed a national cycling team. They practice before dawn on highways to minimize public scrutiny, head scarfs tucked beneath their helmets, and are angling for a spot in the 2016 Olympics.[17]

In the western world, we no longer prevent women from bicycling by rule or by custom, but public policies and infrastructure make it excessively dangerous to get around by bike in many places. As I witness the occasional cyclist pedaling unprotected along the 1960s-era highway near my office—possibly on the way to a low-wage job at one of the big-box outlets that line the commercial strip or to the store to buy clothes or groceries—I am reminded of the inequities that we have built into our cities by making drivers' needs paramount. As Eben Weiss, author of the blog Bike Snob NYC, wrote cogently on this topic recently: "Effectively, we've lost equal access to the public roadways unless we're willing and able to foot the hefty bill for a car."[18] Our car-centric culture disproportionately affects the poor, for whom the costs of owning and operating an automobile are most burdensome. It also disproportionately affects women, who comprise the vast majority of people living in poverty in the U.S. and around the world.[19]

Fortunately, with the proliferation across the country of new infrastructure, laws, and educational campaigns designed to promote bicycling and protect bicyclists, there are important signs of a paradigm shift underway. And it is in many cases women who are in the forefront of advancing this shift.

I am inspired by the likes of Philadelphia's Kristin Gavin, whose nonprofit, Gearing Up, encourages women to bike as a means of working through addiction, trauma, and transitioning back into society following incarceration.[20] Janette Sadik-Khan, the hard-charging former commissioner of New York City's Department of Transportation, who in her tenure helped to implement the nation's largest bike share program, banished cars from Times Square, and oversaw construction of hundreds of miles of new bike facilities.[21] And Veronica Davis, who with her Washington, D.C.-based group, Black Women Bike, is helping to normalize bicycling among a demographic group that has been slow to take to the saddle.[22]

In my own city, they are women like Jennifer Ruley, a civil engineer persistently pushing public works and transportation departments to make streets safer for pedestrians and bicyclists; Karen Parsons, a transportation planner with whom I happen to work who fights for consideration of all modes in every project that comes across her desk; and Tulane University's Liz Davey, who (along with Parsons) was one of the founding members of the New Orleans bicycle advocacy organization now known as Bike Easy back in 2003, a time when very few people here were thinking about the bike as a viable transportation mode. This band of pioneering women also includes Rox'E Homstad who works with the blind and deaf community, is blind and deaf herself, and is quite possibly the most articulate and compelling advocate for safe streets for all that I have ever encountered.

Susan B. Anthony observed during the heyday of the women's suffrage movement that the bicycle was a great emancipator for women. Today, constraints associated with the built environment notwithstanding, I think the bike can be seen as a great equalizer—

a cheap, healthy, accessible mode available to virtually everyone regardless of income, age, race, or gender. I ride alongside janitors and lawyers, parents carting their children to school, and college students on their way to class. They are women, men, young, old, black, white, Asian, and Hispanic.

No matter how much we've paid for our bicycles, what we do for a living or how educated we are, we are all susceptible to the same weather, potholes, and crazy drivers, just as we all know well the joys of navigating our city by bike. While I can't say that I've ever said hello to another driver as I've whizzed down the street in my car, on a mission to get where I'm going as fast as possible, this type of exchange with fellow cyclists occurs every time I ride. From the saddle, one can't help but recognize our common humanity—that we truly are all in this together. It is my hope that this book, in some small way, can help to nudge our society a little bit closer toward that ideal, one pedal stroke at a time.

Getting Started

Choosing a Bike

Cruiser. Cargo. City. Comfort. Racing. Recumbent. Tandem. Touring. The sheer variety of bikes on the market is enough to leave one's head spinning. The good news is that pretty much any of them can get you where you need to go. I would suggest that the best bike to start with is the one that you already have, or the one your nice neighbor has but never uses. If you haven't touched your bike in years, it's not a bad idea to take it by a local bike mechanic to have it checked out first. Like any machine, bikes work best with regular use and maintenance.

In New Orleans, I see 20-somethings pumping along city streets on tricycles. I see a guy who commutes to work solo on a tandem bike, its back seat unoccupied and swaying conspicuously, and I see more than a few adults pedaling around town on children's bikes. For more than a year, I commuted on a beat-up, rusting mountain bike that looked as though it had been salvaged from the junkyard. It made so much noise that people would often turn to look at me as I squeaked down the street, but its clunkiness meant it handled New Orleans' infamous potholes like a champ. Riding that bike also revealed to me exactly what I wanted in a commuter bike; namely, a rack that allowed me to leave behind the heavy bag that was the source of persistent neck pain and back sweat, a frame that allowed me to sit more upright, and fenders to make riding after a rainstorm imminently more feasible.

BIKE BREEDS

Before you head out to the nearest bike shop, think about why and where you want to ride. If you're exclusively interested in getting short distances around town, a cruiser, city bike, or hybrid might be just what you need. On the other hand, if you're looking for a speedier model that you can ride to work during the week and also use on weekends to train for that charity ride you've been contemplating, a touring bike may be more up your alley. If you'll be routinely toting larger loads, you might consider a cargo bike or investing in a bike trailer. Alternatively, those with little to cart around may prefer a simple basket that can be readily installed on the front handlebars of most bikes to accommodate a small bag or purse and carry the added advantage of looking quite adorable.

Some of the Bikes Commonly Used for Commuting

Road bike Anyone who has ever watched the Tour de France or witnessed bands of spandex-clad riders whizzing around the park on a Saturday morning is familiar with this bike type. Your standard road bike is built for speed with a super-light frame and skinny tires. Although it can certainly be used for commuting, this bike type requires a bent-over posture that not all transportation bicyclists will find comfortable or appealing. Moreover, because road bikes are designed with minimal weight in mind, they don't typically accommodate fenders or panniers and their whisper-thin, high-pressure tires tend to be prone to flats.

Cruiser or comfort bike This bike is as at home rolling leisurely along a beach boardwalk as it is well-suited for a trip to the grocery store. It features wider tires than so-called road bikes, and also tends to have a broad, comfortable seat and upright sitting position for relaxed riding. Some cruisers are built with gears, but many models are single-speed. Incidentally, this is my mother's favorite bike type.

Mountain bike Specifically designed for rough terrain, a mountain bike has a thick frame and tires and heavy-duty wheels. Its stout physique makes it great for handling off-road trails, not to mention gravel-strewn and potholed streets.

Touring bike

This road bike variant is a little tougher than most other models use exclusively for fitness or recreational cycling. It provides a more upright sitting posture, and tends to include rack, fender mounts, and handlebars that allow you to rest your hands in a variety of positions to prevent hand, neck, or shoulder discomfort. This can be a good choice for someone interested in commuting to work and logging some serious miles on weekends.

Hybrid bike

The geometry of this bike resembles that of a mountain bike, but with thinner tires, you'll be able to move along at a faster clip. Like comfort bikes, hybrids feature an upright sitting position and comfortable seat.

City or commuter bike

This bike type is built for and marketed to commuters. It tends to feature a sturdy frame and wheels for riding along uneven city streets and a more upright seating position than found on most road bikes to promote comfort and visibility in traffic. It's not meant to be the swiftest in the pack; rather, it is designed as a utilitarian tool for getting you where you need to go. Often, this bike comes equipped with racks and fenders or can be easily outfitted with them.

Cargo bike

Only now catching on in New Orleans, cargo bikes are a fairly common sight on the east and west coasts, and a well-established staple in countries where transportation bicycling is more deeply entrenched. There are numerous variations on the cargo bike. Some are marked by a long tail or front platform to which bulky items may be strapped, and others are characterized by a large bucket into which various items (including kids, pets, groceries, and furniture) may be placed.

SOME OTHER THINGS TO THINK ABOUT IN SELECTING THE RIGHT BIKE

Where You'll Ride

In my flat-as-a-pancake hometown, a single-speed cruiser would probably serve me just fine. Even so, I appreciate the advantage afforded by the three gears on my city bike when I'm climbing the occasional overpass. If you call San Francisco home, you'll definitely want to invest in a bike with more expansive gear capacity to help you push up steep inclines. If the hills where you'll ride are especially onerous, you might even consider a bike equipped with electric-assist.

> *See Changing Gears on page 114 for more about using gears.*

The topography of New Orleans is defined less by hills than by potholes. A sturdy bike with wider tires comes in handy here in helping to ward off deflated tires caused by crashing into one of the ubiquitous craters that line our streets, though there are other steps you can take to minimize the likelihood of flats, such as installing Kevlar-reinforced tires to guard against puncture or high-grade rim strip (the lining that sits between the wheel and tube). No matter what bike type or tires you choose, it's always good to make sure your tires are properly inflated before you ride.

Where You'll Store Your Bike

Unless you have weather-protected outdoor storage space, I wouldn't recommend leaving your new bike outside in the elements. I store my bike on a vertical rack set up in my living room. This means that, up until a recent move to an apartment with ground-level bike storage, I had to lug my bike up and down a set of stairs every time I rode. I adore my steel-frame city bike, but sometimes as I was slogging my bike up the stairs after a long day of work, I wished I'd chosen a lighter model.

What You'll Carry

Acquiring a rear rack and panniers fundamentally changed my bike-riding experience for the better. These simple pieces of equipment allowed me to shed the heavy backpack I used to carry around with me on my bike. They also made it imminently more feasible to bike to the grocery store and to run other errands. Panniers, or saddlebags, attach to or drape over your rack. Many bikes that don't come with racks have the necessary eyelets (also called braze-ons) attached to the frame that will allow you to attach one. Racks to suit many bikes can be picked up relatively inexpensively at most bike stores, though some bikes require brand-specific racks thanks to unconventional sizing.

Your Proportions

Women tend to have proportionally shorter torsos and longer legs than men, and bikes specially-designed for women accommodate these physiological differences. I've ridden a "man's bike" for years without issue, but many women find that bikes built for women suit them more comfortably. Women's bikes (and many European commuter bikes marketed to men) also tend to have a sloped top tube, or step-through, which can make it easier to mount and dismount the bike without kicking the leg over very high, a feature that is especially useful when riding in a skirt.

Any bike store can help you determine the size of bike you require based on your height and stride. A basic test involves standing over the frame. On a bike with a straight top tube, aim for a gap of an inch or two between the top tube and your body. Your saddle height is properly set when you have a slight bend in your leg while the pedal is pushed to its lowest position, closest to the ground.

Your Budget

Your ideal bike may be a $150 secondhand gem from Craigslist or a local refurbishing shop. Or it might be a sleek, aluminum- or carbon-framed showstopper that runs you $1,000 or more. As a very general rule of thumb, chose the best bike available for your particular needs for the money you feel comfortable spending.

Emotion

How did you feel on that bike you tested out at the bike shop last weekend? The first time I road my commuter bike, a chicly simple, steel-gray charmer with matching brown leather bar tape and saddle, I couldn't stop smiling. Gliding down the street, my panniers overflowing with groceries, I felt tall and confident, a bit like I was as pedaling along a European street on a Sunday morning. If you truly like your bike and how you feel on it, you'll be that much more likely to ride.

Saddle (Dis)comfort

As a mostly short-distance commuter bicyclist, for years, my saddle went largely unnoticed. I couldn't have told you much about its practical characteristics; its cool, vintage look and the rich, leathery scent that reminded me of riding horses as a kid were the primary allure of the Brooks saddle my brother gave me as a present one Christmas to replace one that came standard on my bike.

My ignorance of the importance of saddles persisted up until the time I did my first long-distance bike tour. Forty miles in on the first day, my body was fatigued and my hands a little numb, but those sensations barely registered in my mind, which was exclusively focused at the time on the intense burning in my crotch. It felt as though I had scraped one of the most sensitive parts of my anatomy along hot coals. I soon learned that I was by no means alone in succumbing to this type of saddle-born torture, my rookie mistake the result of borrowing a bike that I hadn't bothered testing out until I was out on the road.

Along with your handlebars and pedals, the saddle supports the weight of your body as you ride. It's also the most intimate point of contact between you and your bike. So while the saddle that comes standard may work just fine, if you start to experience discomfort, and especially if you're planning on doing any long-distance riding, you definitely want to pay closer attention to what you're putting between your legs.

For long training rides my friend Christina, a much more avid distance cyclist than I, swears by the Women's Butterfly saddle made by female-centric cycling company Terry. Judging from the online reviews, it seems she's not alone. "I really love it," Christina tells me. "It flexes and has a cut out to relieve pressure where women specifically need it most."

Keep in mind that hugely important to your saddle—and overall bicycling comfort—is the proper fit of your bike.

Even after you're sure your bike is the right size for you, saddles can be raised and lowered, moved front or back, tilted up or down. Other components can similarly be adjusted, and the cumulative result can dramatically affect the way your bike feels. So keep in mind that any discomfort you might experience in the vicinity of your saddle may be remediated by a simple fix. These types of manipulations can be easily done at your local bike shop.

If you're thinking of changing out your saddle, know that there are a multitude of options on the market, many of them specifically designed for women. Many women's saddles are wider in the back to accommodate our typically wider hips and sit bones, and come with a shorter nose (the part that extends between your legs). For those who find chafing on the inner thighs to be a problem, there are saddles with narrower noses, and even a nose-less variety that I've never tried but that some swear by. Moreover, lots of women's saddles come with indentions or cut outs that are designed to accommodate sensitive genital tissues.

Picking out the saddle best suited to your body involves a bit of trial and error. Many bike shops have a variety of saddles in stock that you can try on for size in the store. Some saddle manufacturers, including the women-centric cycling company Terry, offer money-back guarantees that allow you to try out your saddle for a month or so before committing. Gladys Bikes, a women-focused bike shop in Portland, boasts a "saddle library" through which customers can try out as many saddles as they want short-term before making a final purchase. (Unfortunately for those of us who don't live in Portland, this service is limited to in-person customers.)

WHAT TO LOOK FOR

Gladys Bikes owner Leah Benson advises thinking through three main factors in determining the right saddle for you:

1. THE PURPOSE OF YOUR RIDE.

As I learned several hours too late on my first bike tour, the "right saddle" is highly contingent on the type of riding you'll be doing.

2. YOUR SADDLE-TO-HANDLEBAR RELATIONSHIP.

Higher handlebars, which necessitate a more upright seating position, usually require a saddle with a wider rear. On the other hand, if you're riding with your handlebars lowered so that you're in more of a forward-leaning position (as is typically the case on a road bike), a narrower saddle may be appropriate.

3. YOUR BODY.

"Our butts are almost as unique as our thumb prints," Benson says, "and thus saddle fit is deeply personal."

OTHER CONSIDERATIONS

Generally, you'll want to make sure your saddle is wide enough to support your sit bones. This is important because sit bones hanging off the sides of the saddle can mean too much weight bearing down on the soft tissues that lie between. Don't immediately opt for the most cushion-y saddle you find, either. Although a pillowtop saddle may seem ideal, firmer saddles offer more support. "Firm but forgiving" is a good mantra when making your selection. Finally, you might consider a saddle with a cut out or indention designed around the female physique. On the other hand, some people find that these wind up pinching uncomfortably, exacerbating the very problem they are intended to protect against.

TO CUT OUT OR NOT

I found a simple test online (devised by a male bike engineer) purported to aid in assessing the need for a saddle cut out before you even get to the bike shop. Damon Rinard suggests sitting on a wooden or concrete chair or bench and bending at the hips, resting the elbows on the knees. Hold this pose for a few minutes (preferably at a time when your roommate or new romantic interest are not around, as explaining what you're doing could get awkward). If you find that the soft tissues in your crotch are noticeable against the surface in this position, it's likely a cut out will be appropriate for you.

GERKEN'S BIKE SHOP
2803 ST CLAUDE
OPEN 11 AM – 6 PM
CLOSED TUESDAYS
OPEN LATE – NO SPECIAL TIME
CLOSE EARLY – DEPENDS HOW I FEEL
MONDAYS? HMPH!

On the Value of Bike Shops

I recently counted close to two-dozen bike shops operating in New Orleans, a number that has expanded steadily in step with local bicycling interest. There are the stores that specialize in sleek racing bikes and cater to the spandex-clad contingent, and those geared toward the urban commuter, brimming with rugged frames, messenger bags, panniers, and lights made to be spotted from blocks away. There are those that deal in luxury leather saddles and component parts, and bicycle rehab shops where you can buy a remade bike for a steal and even learn to build your own while benefiting disadvantaged youth. There is the one geared toward women's clothing and accessories, several that specialize in rentals and bike tours, purveyors of electric bikes, and the one where I know I can find the perfect Tiki-themed cup holder. And there's the one conveniently located down the street where I'll go for a quick restock of replacement inner tubes even though the prices are higher-than-average and the service less-than-stellar.

I find some reassurance in knowing that no matter where I am in my city, I'm never very far from a bike shop. More so than your average retailer, these businesses are repositories of expertise and experience, places where you can go to get advice about a funny sound your bike is making or to wax nostalgic about 1970s-era English racing bikes, among other esoteric topics. Bike shops attract employees and customers who are passionate about bicycles and people looking to learn more about them, and in this way, I believe they play an essential role in promoting the bike culture of a city. So when you're ready to buy a bike or parts and accessories, consider spending a little bit more and shopping local to support bicycling in your community. Despite the deals to be had online, you don't find this type of knowledge or community on eBay or, for that matter, at your local big box store.

I should note here that, thanks in part to their historic focus on a largely male clientele, some bike shops have developed reputations as rather hostile territory for women. These days, the changing demographics of the bicycling public and a growing awareness of the underserved female market are giving rise to an increasing number of women-owned, women-staffed, or otherwise women-friendly bike shops. So if you don't feel welcomed at your neighborhood bike shop, head elsewhere.

Women on Wheels

"There are these two young fish swimming along, and they happen to meet an older fish swimming the other way, who nods at them and says, 'Morning boys, how's the water?' And the two young fish swim on for a bit, and then eventually one of them looks over at the other and goes, 'What the hell is water?'"
—David Foster Wallace[23]

"If you want to know if an urban environment supports cycling, you can forget about all the detailed 'bikeability indexes'—just measure the proportion of cyclists who are female."
—Jan Garrard, University of Australia[24]

Why Aren't There More (American) Women on Wheels?

There exists in this country a substantial and persistent disparity between the sexes when it comes to willingness to ride a bike. Men consistently outnumber women in U.S. cycling ranks by a ratio of at least two to one, a phenomenon that is not universal among developed nations.[25][26] In countries such as Germany and Denmark, women make nearly as many trips by bike as do men; in the Netherlands, women make up the cycling majority.[27]

The most common explanation for the American bicycling gender gap is a higher risk aversion among women that keeps them out of the saddle. After a century of policies and planning that have heavily favored automobile transportation at the expense of other modes, it is unsurprising that many women—and especially less-experienced riders—consider bicycling to be an unnecessarily dangerous activity.[28]

Their concerns are often warranted. Bicycling is more risky in the U.S. than it is in many other countries.[29] One analysis found a two to three times higher risk of fatality among U.S. cyclists as compared with their counterparts in Holland and Germany, places that boast substantially higher rates of bicycling.[30]

Injury risk tends to decline as cycling rates rise, so in this circular way, even the perceived safety or danger of bicycling in a city may influence actual safety outcomes. The reasons for this safety paradox are unclear, but it would stand to reason that cities that boast large cycling ranks are places where drivers are more aware and respectful of cyclists on the roads, are more likely to be cyclists themselves, and where bicyclists are more apt to be well-educated on the rules of the road. It probably also relates to stronger political clout among cyclists in such communities that helps to ensure cycling-related policy and infrastructure gains.

Generally speaking, more (and more protective) bikeways help to improve cycling safety. In one review of twenty-three international studies on bicycle infrastructure and safety, researchers found that dedicated bike lanes—as opposed to places where bicyclists share the roads with automobile traffic—substantially reduce the risk of injury.[31] (Also important to improving safety for cyclists, the survey found: well-paved bikeways and good nighttime lighting.[32]) In summary, make cycling safer and more women will take to two wheels.

Bicycling tends to be most alluring in places with ample and well-connected bikeways, where the bike offers a convenient way to avoid traffic congestion and parking hassles, and where there are plenty of places to bicycle to—stores, jobs, and other destinations—within close range.

Socioeconomic differences also help to explain the geographic variation in bicycling activity. Access to a car, for example, tends to reduce the changes that a person will use a bike for transportation purposes in this country, while higher income makes it more likely that a person is able to afford the costs of automobile ownership. Similarly, parenthood appears to dampen the chances of bicycling for transportation, especially for women. Even as women now make up close to half of the American workforce, once they become parents, they tend to bear the disproportionate share of child-reading and household responsibilities.[33, 34] Researchers at UCLA estimate that women with children make twice as many trips related to childrearing and household duties like grocery shopping than their male spouses.[35] Bicycling may be a less viable option for these trips, which often involve the transport of goods and passengers. (Though, in the US, the growing popularity and availability of cargo bikes and similar contraptions in use in more heavily biked countries for decades is making these sorts of trips imminently more feasible on bike.[36])

Meanwhile, I think there is a third major contributor to the gender disparity in American bicycling patterns that doesn't get nearly enough attention: the role social forces play in determining a person's willingness to ride a bicycle. I am a strong believer that one's level of exposure to other bicyclists can exert a rather strong enticement or discouragement to getting into the saddle. This idea was underscored for me during research I conducted in 2013, in which I explored some of the reasons behind the substantial discrepancies in transportation behavior observed across my own city—a territory seemingly confronted with nearly identical terrain, weather, and policies.

Experience and Census Bureau data suggest that transportation bicycling is not catching on across New Orleans uniformly. In general, the highest rates of bike commuting, according to American Community Survey estimates, are concentrated along the river in the city's oldest neighborhoods, and also in Mid City, adjacent to City Park and near Bayou St. John. By contrast, bicycle commuting is virtually non-existent across much of New Orleans' post World War II landscape, with a few important exceptions.

I went into my research expecting that those places abuzz with bicyclists were those with physical environments better-suited to the activity—where bike lanes and bike parking were in abundant supply and everyday needs were available in relatively close reach. This assumption was not disproven. As much of the pre-existing research had found and my own study reinforced, there are important correlations between the shape of the physical environment and transportation behavior.

Differences in demographics and the shape of the built environment undoubtedly help to explain the spatial variation in bicycling activity. Access to a car, for example, tends to reduce the chances that a person will use a bike for transportation purposes in this country, while higher income makes it more likely that a person is able to afford the costs of automobile ownership. Similarly, parenthood appears to dampen the chances of a bicycling for transportation.

But over the course of my study, I became increasingly intrigued by the more difficult-to-measure reasons why people might or might not opt for the mode.

"It makes me feel like an asshole, living in Bywater and driving," my friend Daisy told me one evening over drinks at a wine bar on St. Claude Avenue, in a section of town just downriver from the French Quarter that is one of the most-biked in the city. We sat in a window fronting the avenue, watching as a steady stream of bicyclists whizzed by on the bike lane installed along three miles of the corridor in 2008. She explained that she had long been accustomed to driving most places, but after relocating to Bywater, she suddenly felt self-conscious about her transportation habits in light of the bicyclists she encountered in her new neighborhood with great frequency.

By contrast, a woman I interviewed who lived in Navarre, part of suburban Lakeview, told me that she never thought twice about jumping in her car to get everywhere she needed to go. She struggled to recall a time when she, her husband, and their small child had gotten anywhere by some means other than driving, the occasional walk around the block for exercise notwithstanding. Driving presented the most convenient and safest option, she told me, thanks in no small part to the ease with which she was able to drive and park in and around her neighborhood. She also noted the dearth of destinations within close range, though she admitted that even if there were a greater number of stores or restaurants nearby, she probably wouldn't bike to them.

It struck me that this woman's auto-centric choices might be rooted as much in the cultural environment of her neighborhood as was Daisy's self-consciousness about driving through hers. Surrounded mostly by people who grab their car keys every time they head out the door, she wasn't likely to feel compelled to consider other options.

After all, it isn't as though bicycling from Navarre required some Herculean effort. To test the ease of bicycling from each of the neighborhoods, I mapped and bicycled a route roughly from the center of Bywater and Navarre to a spot near the center of New Orleans' Central Business District, the site of one of the highest concentrations of jobs in the region. To my surprise, the trip from Navarre was only about a mile longer than the trip from Bywater. By some measures, it was a more enjoyable ride.

Two studies I came across over the course of my research lend support to the influence of peer pressure on our individual transportation behavior. Portland-based researchers Jennifer Dill and Kim Voros concluded in their 2007 analysis that the bicycling behavior of neighbors, coworkers, and friends exerts substantial sway over a person's bicycling interest and habits.[37] If a place is teeming with cyclists, bicycling may be more readily perceived as viable, safe, and socially acceptable. In places where little bicycling occurs, the opposite perception likely holds true. In a separate survey of Portland-area adults, Dill and her research associate Nathan McNeill found that those who reported they did not bicycle were less likely to live or work with people who did so, or to see "people who look like them cycling on city streets."[38]

By no means do I intend to minimize the importance of the built environment in fueling or dampening transportation bicycling interest and improving safety. What I am suggesting is that there seems to be an element of contagiousness involved in transportation behavior, and that as more women hop into the saddle, more women will see the bike as a viable transportation option. I also believe that by providing a physical environment more conducive to bicycling—one with proper infrastructure, education, and compatible land use and parking policies—policy makers can help to create the conditions in which bicycling is likely to thrive.

So what is it about places like Germany, The Netherlands, and Denmark that has given rise to the type of gender equity in bicycling that evades the U.S. at present? These countries boast high and growing rates of bicycling among all segments of society thanks in part to decades-in-the-making policies and programs that provide safe, well-connected bikeways, connectivity to transit, and extensive and early safety training for cyclists and drivers.[39] They are also places in which driving and parking are expensive, thanks to higher fuel costs and vehicle taxes, and where the physical form resulting from their people-oriented layouts, with well-connected, pedestrian-scale streets, and mix of uses necessitated by their pre-car origins, make getting to day-to-day necessities relatively easy to accomplish by foot.

Moreover, recent research out of UCLA suggests that there's another, often overlooked, part of the transportation equation that could help to explain why some European women bike so much more than their American counterparts: social policies that help parents juggle the competing demands of life and parenthood more easily.[40] In the Netherlands, for instance, researchers found that flextime, paternity leave and shorter workweeks allow for child rearing to be handled more equitably by both parents.[41] (Single parents are another matter, but I have no doubt single mothers in parts of Western Europe have an easier go at things than do single mothers in the U.S., along a number of important metrics. France, for example, offers affordable, government-subsidized childcare, something many parents I know in the U.S. can only dream about.) Meantime, neighborhood schools still abound alongside safe and efficient walking and biking infrastructure, allowing children much more independence when it comes to getting themselves around.[42]

Riding in Less Than Ideal Conditions

RIDING AT NIGHT

Although I know lots of people who do it without qualms or incident, I'm personally not a big fan of biking alone at night in my city, given my reliance on high-traffic routes that lack dedicated bikeways and my city's unusual crime problem. That said, there are occasions in which I end up biking after dark, whether because a meeting runs late, I get lost in conversation with friends, or because I want to catch the last song of a favorite band at Jazz Fest. In these instances, I take even more precautions than usual to ensure that I make it home safely.

This sometimes means going out of my way to take a route that features dedicated bikeways, lots

Getting Back on the Bike

This book assumes some basic level of comfort with riding a bike. If you haven't been on a bike since elementary school or you feel uncertain about your skill, be sure to practice the basics of bicycle riding—maneuvers such as getting on and off the bike, balancing, pedaling, starting, stopping, and steering—before heading out on the road.

Start out in a park or on very low-traffic residential streets until you regain your confidence. You might even recruit a more experienced friend to ride with you and help you get the hang of things. Begin slowly, perhaps starting with easy laps around a protected section of a park or an empty parking lot, working your way up to a short trip to your neighborhood coffee shop or some other close-by locale. Gradually increase your range as you get more comfortable.

If you've never ridden a bike, or your think you need more intensive instruction, look for adult bicycling classes now offered in a growing number of cities. Check online or with your local bicycle-advocacy organization to find classes near you.

of lighting, or slow-moving traffic. One of the most important pieces of advice I can offer for riding after dark is one that also applies in well-lit situations: do everything you can to be visible to drivers. Good lights are essential, and reflective, light-colored clothing and accessories are also really good ideas. I recently acquired a neon yellow trench coat with reflector flaps that can be pulled out of the arms when biking. Wearing it, I look a little like a school-crossing guard, but I'm pretty hard to miss.

When riding at night, I'm also more likely to take the lane to improve the chances that I'll be spotted by drivers coming up from behind me. Other times, where there is a wide shoulder or an unoccupied parking lane available, I'll ride in that space if I feel more comfortable doing so. Note that shoulders often tend to be places where tube-slitting debris accumulates, and riding in and out of a parking lane can make it less likely for drivers to see you or be able to predict your movements.

My Final Tips for Riding at Night:

• Stick to roads that you know to make it less likely that you'll encounter an unexpected pothole or other hazard or inadvertently ride through a shaky part of town

• Listen to your instincts. If you're not comfortable bicycling for whatever reason, find another way home.

The Importance of Good Lights

Even after you make sure that drivers have no choice but to see you, ride as if they don't. This is a good tip for riding any time of day or night. I am continuously puzzled by the number of people I see riding the streets after dark with no lights and dark clothing like ninjas darting through the night. I assume these cyclists expect that because they are able to see well enough to navigate the roads, drivers will have no trouble spotting them. But as someone who is on high alert for fellow cyclists while driving, I know well that this is not the case. On more than one occasion, a member of this un-illuminated tribe has materialized from the shadows into the very space where I am about to open my car door or pull from a parallel parking space.

Nighttime and other low-light situations are where high-quality lights come in most handy. At a minimum, you'll want a strong front light that emits white light and a red light for the back. In some places, this is the standard equipment required by law. I sometimes strap a third blinking LED light to the back of my helmet or torso to improve the chances I'll be spotted.

The brighter the better when it comes to your lights. Look for a headlight with a minimum 100 lumens. I recently got a 400-lumen front light that lights up the road in front of me like a spotlight. As a bonus, it emits a flicker of light from the sides so that drivers approaching at intersections are more likely to notice me. It's also rechargeable, so I don't have the excuse of not having any extra batteries lying around when it starts to go dim.

I think it's important to put the threat of crime into some perspective. For one thing, rates of violent crime are on the decline across the U.S., despite what the cable news channels might be screaming.[43] For another, even as women tend to feel more vulnerable to crime than do men, I was surprised to learn recently that men are actually more likely to fall victim to violent criminal activity than are women, statistically speaking.[44]

Researchers have dubbed this contradiction the "gender-fear paradox," and some believe that women's disproportionate fear of all types of violent crime could stem from our increased susceptibility to sexual assault (admittedly, a very significant exception to the crime-vulnerability calculation).[45] I'm not sure that this information substantially alters my feelings about my safety in public spaces, but it at least offers me a modicum of reassurance as I'm out riding my bike or walking to the grocery store.

Meantime, there are a few basic steps I take when riding my bike to help minimize my vulnerability.

When I first started riding, I tended to favor very low-traffic roadways, especially at night. It was great having the streets all to myself until I realized I actually didn't. I learned the drawbacks of my ride-where-the-people-aren't approach the hard way several years ago while riding through a dimly-lit, quiet part of town. Before I knew what was happening, three gun-toting teenagers appeared from out of nowhere and surrounded me. Fortunately, they only took a wallet and left my friend and me (and our bikes) alone.

Scary as it was, that experience taught me an important lesson about the value of "eyes on the street," to borrow a phrase coined by the late Jane Jacobs. It also changed how I ride my bike. When riding, especially at night but even during the day in some instances, I now stick to more heavily-traveled routes, taking care that my bike is well-lit and that my clothing is light-colored and reflective. Riding more heavily-traveled streets for safety's sake may seem counterintuitive, but I feel most comfortable balancing traffic concerns with other factors.

My friend Tricia bikes at night far more often than I. She advises paying special attention around intersections, trees and other vegetation for people who might be obscured by the shadows, and continuously scanning one's surroundings.

"If I pass someone, I always try to make eye contact and offer a friendly, 'How are you?' in the hopes that they'll see me as something more than a wallet," she told me. Tricia also avoids taking out her cell phone while riding (smart phones are a prime target of thieves where we live, to say nothing of the distraction they offer the user) and she tries not to carry any unnecessary baggage. Tricia also totes pepper spray on her nighttime rides, attaching it with a carabiner to the strap of her messenger bag or to a belt loop, and she stows a compact U-lock in her back pocket as her wardrobe allows, which she figures could be employed to defend herself. Fortunately, she's never had to use either of these tools.

RIDING IN THE RAIN

Along with heat and humidity, another less-than-ideal weather phenomenon that many bicyclists are certain to confront at some point is rain. In the staggering heat of summer, a brief storm can feel like tiny bits of Manna raining down in response to the prayers of a sweaty, desperate citizenry. But when you're halfway to work on your bike and the skies open up, it can feel a lot like divine retribution. I'm reassured by knowing that notoriously rainy cities including Portland and Seattle boast some of the highest bike-commute rates in the country. Clearly, there are workarounds.

Because New Orleans weather is often unpredictable, I've learned to pack a rain poncho on my bike even on days when the forecast calls for clear skies, and to bring along a plastic baggie or waterproof container in case I need to protect my phone from an unexpected deluge.

Don't forget that even if you've covered the top half of your body with a poncho or waterproof jacket, your lower half is very much exposed to the elements when you're riding a bike. A pair of rain pants or another type of lower-body covering can make riding in the rain much more bearable. Similarly, if you live in an especially rainy climate, you might consider a pair of neoprene shoe covers to help keep your feet dry.

Because there are few worse feelings to me than wearing shoes soaked through to my socks, a pair of rubber flip flops are my go-to when rain is likely, and also my preferred footwear when biking in the summer. (A drawback of flip flops in the rain is that they tend to get slippery when wet and risk sliding off the pedals.) I recently came across a pair of rain-proof ballet flats that may be my next bike-related purchase. They would be equally suitable for slogging through puddles or paired with a skirt for work.

Clothing aside, lights and bright-colored or reflective clothing are crucial when riding in the rain, when drivers' visibility can be sorely compromised and when they may not expect to encounter cyclists in the roads.

KNOW WHEN TO CALL IT A DAY

There are times when biking in the rain is manageable and even quite pleasant. I've had some truly invigorating afternoons biking home in a light mist after a long day in the office. But there have also been times when the rain has been so heavy as to make my journey treacherously unsafe. It's important to trust your instincts. Sometimes, you need to just lock up your bike and find another option. Here are a few that I've found helpful:

- Check the radar for a lull in the rain and wait it out in a dry place.
- Take transit. Transit vehicles in many cities are bike-friendly. In New Orleans, our buses are equipped with bike racks that anyone can use so long as there's adequate space. Our streetcars are another story. Call a cab or rideshare service. In some cities, these cars are outfitted with bike racks.
- Call a friend who has a bike rack on her car. If she's a bicyclist, she'll likely appreciate the positive bike karma and be glad to pick you up. Just don't forget to reciprocate.

Dealing with Harassment

WHAT TO DO WHEN DRIVERS DON'T RESPECT YOUR RIGHT TO THE ROAD

It's pretty much inevitable. Once you start riding your bike in the streets with any frequency, you will find yourself growing increasingly indignant about the poor skills and general lack of awareness and courtesy exhibited by a strikingly high proportion of drivers in your city. You will eventually get honked at, yelled at, and possibly even run off the road.

There is, I have found, a breed of driver that acts with impunity from the comfort and anonymity provided by their automobile. They believe their status aboard their two-ton steel and glass bubble renders them ruler of the roadways. It is as though in getting into the driver's seat, they are immediately divorced from the rest of humanity.

The other day, I got flipped off by an old man who apparently didn't believe I deserved to share the street with his Toyota Corolla. Another time, a mom with her two young kids in tow nearly plowed into me; she was so busy flailing her arms, honking her horn, and yelling at me to "get in the bike lane," by which she ostensibly meant the sidewalk, where it is illegal to ride in my city for those of us older than fourteen.

Fortunately, as more and more people are taking to the streets by bike, I find myself confronted by this type of driver with noticeably less frequency. Most days, I make the sixteen-mile round trip between my apartment and my office without a single negative encounter. But occasionally, I'll come across a driver whose ignorance, audacity and sheer irresponsibility makes me scream. Literally. Though often, said driver remains blithely unaware of ever being in the wrong.

Cyclists have a variety of ways of dealing with bad driver behavior. Some respond with cool indifference, carrying on as though nothing were amiss. One of my friends flashes an unexpected peace sign. Another blows kisses. I've known others to chase down offending drivers and let loose on them a tirade of expletives and even physical aggression. (I generally find that this latter type of response, though immediately quite gratifying, is not at all effective in changing bad behavior or in convincing an offender that they are acting inappropriately, to say nothing of the dangers entailed. Instead, responding to unseemly behavior in kind carries a high risk of proving to the driver, and anyone else who might be watching, that *you* are in fact the asshole.)

I think that one of the best ways to improve driver behavior is to simply ride a bike and encourage others to do so too. This may seem overly simplistic, with a frustratingly incremental payoff, but getting more people biking on the streets will over time make drivers more accustomed to anticipating and looking out for cyclists. It also improves the likelihood that drivers are themselves cyclists, and every cyclist I know who gets into a driver's seat is much more understanding, aware, and patient than your average motorist.

It's helpful to come up with a plan for handling bad driver behavior so that you're less likely to be totally flustered—or driven to act irrationally—when you encounter it.

Lately, when I hear someone honking at me, I turn (assuming I can do this safely) and look the driver straight in the face. In looking the driver in the eye, I am better able to gauge the riskiness of the situation. Sometimes, I realize that the person was simply a friend trying to get my attention. But other times, it's clear that the intention is to get me out of the way. If a driver is displaying reckless behavior, I move out of the way as quickly as possible. But often, this very simple gesture has a remarkable disarming effect. I've seen exasperated motorists turn red and cower in embarrassment just by virtue of this very human exchange.

I find that I'm often in a position to speak with a driver who is ignorant of my rights to the road. With hilarious frequency, the driver who was so very impatient to speed past me, in the process violating all manner of road rules and common courtesy, ends up stopped by the closest traffic light. This sometimes provides for the perfect chance to glide right up to the driver's window and engage in a brief exchange.

You might come up with a brief script that you can employ should you be afforded a similar opportunity. Here's a sample template: Excuse me (sir/ma'am). I understand that you are frustrated, but I think it might be helpful to point out that the law gives me every right to ride here and says you are supposed to leave ample space when passing me. I know that you are in a hurry, but just keep in mind that your hurry affects my life. Thanks (BIG SMILE)!

I can't claim that this tactic has resulted in any dramatic shifts in perspective among the motoring public. It has, however, given me the satisfaction of knowing I've stated my case and hopefully helped to discourage similar bad behavior in the future.

A few months ago, I was riding home when the driver of an SUV pulled up next to me and rolled down his window. I started to tense up, readying myself for a showdown. "Get on the sidewalk!" I expected to hear. "You're slowing down traffic!" I almost didn't believe what I heard instead. "You're my hero!" a woman's voice shouted as she carefully accelerated past me. I smiled the rest of the way home.

HOW TO HANDLE GENDER-BASED STREET HARASSMENT

For many women, jeers, unsolicited reviews of body parts, and sexual advances from strangers are a regular (and dreaded) part of stepping out of the door. For some, just the anticipation of this type of street harassment is enough to cause a reconfiguring of day-to-day routines, whether it means avoiding a particular road or intersection, pulling an otherwise unnecessary skirt over a favorite pair of yoga pants, or driving the two blocks to the store.

The group Stop Street Harassment (www.stopstreetharassment.org) estimates that two-thirds of all women in the U.S. have dealt with some form of sexual harassment on the street. This includes a range of experiences, from getting whistled or honked at to even being grabbed or followed. "A lot of times it's honking, guys sticking their head out the window and staring at you as they drive by," said Vanessa Smith, a New Orleans bike commuter.

Smith works with the New Orleans chapter of the anti-street-harassment organization Hollaback!, a group now in operation in cities around the globe that has as its mission combatting the catcalls, vulgar commentary, and related activity that many women contend with simply by virtue of their presence in the public sphere. (Women are not alone in being confronted with this behavior, say the experts, but along with gay and transgendered people, bear the disproportionate brunt of it.)

For some of us, the bike can function as a sort of street harassment escape valve, providing for a measure of detachment and a means of escape from potentially uncomfortable and even dangerous situations. If nothing else, the speed advantage afforded by a bike relative to walking minimizes the chances of overhearing unwelcomed editorializing —and makes it easier to get away from it.

"If someone decides to yell something at me, I feel a lot less vulnerable on a bike," said Katie Monroe, who works for the Bicycle Coalition of Greater Philadelphia. Monroe founded the group Women Bike PHL and has testified before the Philadelphia City Council on the subject of street harassment and bike harassment more specifically, arguing that the phenomena make our streets less hospitable places for certain groups of people. "Sometimes," she added, "I even feel safe enough to yell something back at them, which I never do when I'm walking."

There are, of course, innumerable ways to react should you be confronted by a harasser. Stop Street Harassment's website offers a host of information on the subject, including a breakdown of pertinent laws by state and tips for responding to perpetrators. (Maintain eye contact. Exude calm and confidence. Don't swear or lose your temper.)

As someone who always comes up with the witty retort five minutes too late, I think it's useful to have a repertoire of responses in mind for the next time a guy you don't know lobs a "Nice ass, baby" or "I wish I was that saddle" your way.

My friend Jessie once sobbed "My dad just died!" to a fellow pedestrian after he instructed her to "Smile, beautiful" as she passed him in the street. The perpetrator apologized immediately and effusively. Her father, it should be said, was very much alive.

A Note of Caution

Smith stresses that your safety should always be paramount in determining how best handle a harasser. Be sure to follow your gut and remove yourself from any situation in which you feel as though you may be in danger.

For times when the perfect rejoinder doesn't roll smoothly off your tongue—or you feel uncomfortable faking the death of a loved one as part of a comeback—you might deploy one of the following five strategies, which may be applied alone or in combination:

1. Ignore him. I imagine your typical street harasser is looking to get some type of response from his target. After all, this type of situation probably presents him with a rare chance for female attention and interaction. So try not giving it to him.

2. Raise your pinky. If the tried and true middle finger extension seems too vulgar or trite, try waving your pinky finger in the direction of your harasser. Even if he doesn't get it right away, it may just leave him so confused as to shut him up. This move is inspired by an Australian ad campaign designed to teach young men that women don't like guys who speed. Although the pinky wave may not be fully understood by the U.S. populace, I think it's high time the gesture took hold here. (Note: I have not done exhaustive research into what connotations this move may hold in some other cultures, so use your discretion and/or local expertise.)

3. Report it. If the harassment occurs in or near a business, public facility, or transit vehicle, let the business owner or relevant public agency know.

4. Let a card do the talking. Some advocacy groups have started propagating what Hollaback! dubs "creeper cards," which a woman can hand over to her harasser to let him know his behavior is unacceptable. You can download these cards from various websites or make some of your own and, when harassment strikes, dole them out silently, then walk or bike away.

5. Document it. If you can do so safely, you might try taking a picture or a video of your harasser and/or uploading your harassment story to your social media outlet of choice. Hollaback! has a smart phone app available in a number of cities (see ihollaback.org) that allows users to log the location and type of street harassment encountered, and the group's website invites visitors to share their experiences. If the harassment is especially egregious, you may also be able to use this as evidence to hand over to the police.

Monroe, for her part, tends to take a more zen-like approach lately when confronted with street harassment. "Engaging," she said, "usually makes me angrier."

Riding with a Child

As a childless woman who, for the most part, is responsible only for myself, I can only imagine how much more complicated life in general, not to mention my commuting patterns,  would be if I had kids to contend with. It's one thing for me to plan to leave a little early and ride my bike to work. If I had to get myself and two children ready, take them each to school, and pick up groceries and the dry cleaning on the way home, taking my bike might not be a very practical option. And that's not even getting to the safety concerns.

Because the U.S. hasn't in recent history done a great job of prioritizing safe provisions for bicyclists and pedestrians, and because our car-oriented culture has built cities in which it is necessary to travel great distances to accomplish everyday needs, it's no wonder that many people don't consider the bike a viable transportation option. It's even more understandable that they are reluctant to place their progeny in harm's way.

Some of my friends would eagerly point to statistics here proving that cars—one of the top sources of injury and death in the U.S.—are far from risk-free. While this is certainly true, I'll be the last one to suggest that a parent do anything that they believe places their child at risk.

Yet as a relatively well-functioning adult who spent the earliest part of my life 30-some years ago being shuttled between home and my babysitter's house in the sturdy plastic seat attached to the back of my mom's Trek, I'd like to believe that I'm living proof that it is possible to effectively transport children on bikes, even in less-than-ideal environments. (Baton Rouge, Louisiana, where I grew up, is hardly a bastion of bike-friendliness, though things are starting to change for the better.) Looking back on it, I think those earliest experiences biking around with my mom helped to instill in me a lifetime love of the outdoors and of exercise and allowed us to connect in a really special way.

I have been inspired by many other examples of women—and men—who find a way to bike with their kids, even in the most sprawling, auto-centric cities.

St. Charles Avenue in New Orleans is known for its stately old mansions and the iconic green streetcar running beneath the avenue's canopy of sprawling live oaks. More recently, and especially in light of a bike lane that was striped along the avenue a couple years ago, it has become a case study in the art of bike commuting. *On any given weekday, you can find the full spectrum of bike commuters on display along the avenue.* There are suited up business people with briefcases slung across their backs, tattooed hipsters making their way to a coffee shop or to class, and maintenance workers headed to manicure lawns, impressively balancing edging tools, clippers and blowers on their bikes. And if you pay attention long enough to the parade of cyclists making use of the avenue, you'll spot among them a fair number of parents transporting their children to or from school or daycare.

There's the toned woman in workout clothes who pedals her three sons to school every morning, the littlest in a trailer attached to his mother's bike and the other two on bikes of their own. There's the man biking with his ten-year-old daughter settled comfortably in the rear saddle of their tandem. There are parents riding with younger children strapped into seats attached to the fronts and backs of their bikes. Increasingly common is the eye-catching, fluorescent green variety that mounts to the front, which I've heard from friends who swear by this model makes it easier to talk to a child—and keep closer watch over what they're up to.

One Saturday morning, I was out for a run when I spotted a sight I'd never seen before in New Orleans. A mother, steering with one hand so she could sip her coffee, pedaled a Dutch-style cargo bike along the avenue, her two toe-headed boys sitting contentedly in the oversized bucket in front. I broke into a sprint to snap a picture of this scene with my cell phone, feeling the excitement I imagine a veteran bird watcher experiences upon catching a glimpse of a new species for the first time.

The general rule of thumb dispensed by the American Academy of Pediatrics is to wait until kids are at least a year old before putting them on a bike, in part to ensure their necks are strong enough to support a helmet. But my sister-in-law Stephanie started biking with her daughter, Ella, when Ella was just six months old. It was in part an act of desperation.

On Kids' Helmets

Getting a child to wear a helmet can be a challenging endeavor, and your kid is not likely to be won over to having a stiff, awkward object strapped to her head by an erudite discussion of safety statistics. (This strategy doesn't seem to be that effective in convincing many adults, either.) My sister-in-law Stephanie Jones Jordan has a few suggestions for making helmet-wearing less of a struggle:

1. Choose wisely. The array of kids' helmets on the market allows for lots of options, but in selecting the best model for your child, consider how and where it will be worn. An irregularly shaped helmet made with aerodynamics or novelty in mind (built-in Mohawks and animal ears are popular lately) may be great for a child who is riding solo, but can make reclining or napping difficult. A better option may be one of the so-called urban bicycling helmets. These tend to be lower-profile and uniformly shaped, making resting the head against the back of a trailer or child seat more comfortable.

2. Involve your child in picking out her helmet. "If she loves her helmet, she'll like to wear it," Stephanie advises.

3. Consistency is key. If your child knows she's expected to wear her helmet every time you get on the bike, convincing her to do so will become less and less of a fight over time.

In her early days, Ella rarely slept through the night. She also hated riding in a car. On the occasions when travel was impossible except by getting in a car, Ella would scream until it seemed like she couldn't possibly have any energy left in her miniature body, then she'd scream some more.

Stephanie discovered almost by accident that placing her tiny daughter in a bike trailer (she'd secure Ella in a car seat attached inside) had the almost magical effect of calming her ceaselessly energetic, sleep-resistant child to the point that she would actually take a nap. As a bonus, it allowed Stephanie to get in some much-needed exercise and to connect with the outside world. As a newly minted stay-at-home-mom accustomed to the regular interaction that comes with the working world, for the first six months of her daughter's life, my sister-in-law felt rather isolated. But once she figured out Ella's comfort on a bike, Stephanie discovered she could ride for two, three, even four hours with her daughter strapped contentedly in her bike trailer, warm and dry, even on the rainy days in Seattle where they live.

"Once I realized that Ella was happy in a trailer, I felt like I had instant freedom," Stephanie told me. She eventually worked up to biking with her daughter in tow as often as five times a week.

Riding with her daughter, now three, requires a little more planning than it does when Stephanie rides alone. When she's biking with Ella, Stephanie sticks to low-traffic residential roads and separated bike facilities, avoiding riskier routes that she feels perfectly comfortable riding alone. She also spends some time figuring out how to shorten the time traveled between places and avoid the big hills whose challenge she otherwise welcomes. Kids, Stephanie points out, can add a lot of extra weight to your ride, especially when you add diaper bags, blankets, snacks, toys and groceries.

Stephanie recently gave birth to her second child, a daughter named Audrey, and Ella has graduated from her trailer to a child seat attached to the back of the bike. When the new baby reaches six months or so, it's Stephanie's plan to bike with both of her daughters, Audrey taking the seat her big sister once occupied in the car seat carefully strapped into the bike trailer.

Why Your Bike Commute Means You Can Spend Less Time at the Gym

I recently took part in an online contest sponsored by the League of American Bicyclists that for five months challenged participants to track every mile they rode on their bikes. Bicyclists earned points for days they rode at least one mile and were pushed further up in the rankings the more days—and more miles—they accumulated.

One of the devices used to keep participants motivated was an online tracker that estimated pounds of carbon saved from the atmosphere by bicycling instead of driving. Another tallied money saved in gas. Still another tracked how many calories the rider had burned by opting to bike to get where she needed to go.

It felt good seeing the hundreds of pounds of carbon dioxide I'd kept from the atmosphere by riding my bike, and the $45 in gas money I'd saved by the end of the first month allowed me to better rationalize my designer coffee habit. To my dismay, the one tool I never got working was the one that measured calories burned. As I watched others on the leaderboard rack up many McDonald's meals worth of miles ridden, my calorie tracker rested perennially and frustratingly on zero.

I've long believed that apart from providing proper infrastructure and policies that make the streets safer, one of the best ways to get more people motivated to ride their bikes would be to better advertise the immediate personal advantages of bicycling.

Most of us are aware on some level aware of the environmental merits of riding a bike—that by opting for two wheels over four, we can reduce the greenhouse gases and other pollutants sent into the atmosphere, minimize consumption of a non-renewable resource, and alleviate congestion on the streets. Yet with the scale of the ecological challenges we confront so vast and the consequences far enough removed from our day-to-day lives, I think it's become easy for us as a culture to minimize the significance of our deeply engrained driving habits, among other behaviors that are contributing to our global climate problem.

Health benefits, on the other hand, seem to me some of the most readily relatable perks of cycling. We are a nation obsessed with our weight, as evidenced by the billions of dollars we spend every year on gym memberships, diet drugs, and other assorted mechanisms for whittling our ever-expanding waistlines.

Simultaneously, we spend countless hours (and billions of gallons of gasoline) stuck in our cars in traffic. Know how many calories you expend sitting in your car on your way to work? Me neither, but I can assure you that it's not very many.

I think everyone recognizes intuitively that bicycling, like most forms of physical activity, is good for you. But I don't think many of us recognize just how substantial the benefits of transportation bicycling can be. An expanding body of research supports what those of us who ride our bikes regularly know well: that urban bicycling promotes cardiovascular health, reduces stress, and improves cognitive function. Several studies have also found that the health benefits of bicycling substantially outweigh the risks, including increased vulnerability in

Fueling Your Ride

The rise of the personal automobile has in many ways made life more convenient. But the car has also made our cities more spread out, our streets more congested and our lives vastly more sedentary than ever before. At a time when the World Health Organization estimates one in three adults worldwide fails to get enough exercise, the bike can be an ideal antidote to inactivity, a simple tool to incorporate movement into your daily life while getting you where you need to go.[47]

Consider this:

- A 155-pound person bicycling at a moderate pace of 12-13.9 miles per hour burns approximately 480 calories in an hour, according to estimates compiled by Harvard Medical School.[48] That's more calories per hour than would be expended in a typical aerobics class, elliptical workout, or swift walk.

- By biking four miles to work and back at a moderate pace just twice a week, over the course of a month, the average American woman would burn the caloric equivalent of almost a pound of fat.[49]

traffic crashes and exposure to air pollution.[46]

Trading your car for your bike, even occasionally, can also help you fit into your favorite pair of skinny jeans without a whole lot of effort. My bike ride to work burns more calories than I do on my typical morning run. It means I'm getting good exercise doing something I have to do anyway, and having lots more fun than most people stuck behind the wheel!

Certainly, calories burned while biking vary quite substantially depending on how fast and far you ride, among other variables. But as my office mates kvetch about having to go to spinning class after a long day at the office, I can't help but take some satisfaction in knowing my activity quota has been met for the day by simply getting to and from the office at a relatively leisurely pace.

I am reminded of a bit of especially cogent guerilla advocacy that made its way around the internet a couple years ago. It was a simple stencil featuring a bike and a car side-by-side. "This one runs on fat and saves you money," the text above the bike read. "This one runs on money and makes you fat," read the caption above the car. I sometimes think about that graphic as I'm filling up my car with gas. Smelling the noxious fumes and watching the price tally tick ever higher, I wish I'd ridden my bike.

Stretching, strengthening, and injury-prevention

I am not anything close to a healthcare professional, and it is by no means the aim of this book to dispense medical advice. Even so, I think it's a good idea for anyone who rides a bike to be equipped with a basic understanding of some possible sources of discomfort associated with the activity and ways to prevent and treat common aches and pains.

One of the virtues of bicycling is that it is a low-impact form of exercise that can be done by almost anyone. So it was much to my surprise that not long after I started riding to work with regularity, I developed a nagging pain in my left knee. I've been a runner for years, and had never experienced any similar episodes.

After some x-rays and evaluation, a sports medicine doctor diagnosed patellofemoral syndrome, more commonly known as "runners' knee," which is apparently one of the most frequently occurring sports-related injuries. It was the result, he told me, of hyper-developed quadriceps, relatively weak gluteal muscles, and super-tight hamstrings and hips created by both of my favorite forms of exercise. To my relief, he advised me to continue running and biking and he prescribed physical therapy to improve my strength and flexibility.

Conveniently for me, my mother-in-law, Danni Jones, is a physical therapist. After my diagnosis, from her vacation post in the mountains, Danni whipped out a series of smart phone videos demonstrating exercises I could do to correct the problem.

"Even though bicycling is a great, low-impact activity, I see a good share of injuries associated with it," she tells me. "It's the repetitive movement. The muscles most frequently used become tight and others that are underutilized may become weak, creating imbalances around the joints that lead to injury and pain."

Selecting the right bike for your body and having it fit to your frame can minimize injury, as can preventative exercises, especially stretches to loosen tight hamstrings, hip flexors, and IT bands, and those that strengthen the gluteal muscles and core.

Step-up *Strengthens gluteal muscles, reinforces proper knee alignment.*

Standing on a small step with your feet facing forward, raise one leg a few inches and bend the standing leg so that the foot of your lifted leg moves toward the floor. Engage the gluteal muscles of your standing leg and don't let your knee move significantly past your toes. Now straighten your standing leg. Repeat about twenty times, switch legs and do another set on each leg. In doing this exercise, be sure that the sit bone, center of the knee, and third toe are in alignment with one another and don't let the knee of your standing leg bend in toward your big toe.

Single-leg Bridge *Strengthens gluteal muscles, hamstrings and core.*

Begin on your back with your knees bent and your feet flat on the floor. Engaging your gluteal and abdominal muscles, lift your hips straight up to form a line between your shoulders and knees. Keeping your hips raised and your torso and pelvis lined up, straighten one leg, keeping your knees in the same plane and your trunk level. Hold for five seconds, lower and repeat. Aim for two sets of about ten repetitions on each leg.

Single-leg Dead Lift *Strengthens gluteals and hips, helps with trunk stability, coordination, and balance.*

Begin in a standing position with a slight bend in your knees. Holding a dumbbell or barbell in front of you and engaging the gluteal muscles of your standing leg, bend one leg then lower your weights and torso toward the floor as you lift the bent leg behind you, creating an arc with your torso and leg. Raise your torso and lower your leg. Repeat about ten times and switch sides. Aim for two sets of ten on each leg.

This one takes some practice, so don't feel bad if you don't get it right away. You might begin with no weights, adding weights on as your strength and coordination improve. Another modification that can help you get the hang of this exercise is to put your foot against a wall and press into it as you lean into the position.

The Good Witch *Helps to improve bike posture to combat neck, lower back and shoulder pain.*

Hunching over your handlebars for extended periods of time can lead to lower back, neck and shoulder pain. When riding, aim to bend forward at the hips with the spine aligned, your hips in as neutral a position as possible, without any arch or tuck in your pelvis. You can get a feel for proper bike posture by grabbing a broom stick and placing it between your shoulder blades, vertical to the floor. Lean forward slightly from your hips, pulling in your abdominals and pushing your torso against the stick. With your legs hip width apart, bend your knees, making sure they don't go past your toes, to get a better sense for how this feels on the bike.

The Clam *Strengthens muscles around the hip.*

Lying on one side, with your head resting on your arm flat on the floor or

in the palm of your hand with your arm bent, bend your knees to a 90-degree angle. Keep your feet pressed together as you rotate the knee of the top leg toward the ceiling, squeezing your gluteal muscles. Aim for two sets of twenty repetitions on each side.

The Superman *Strengthens the shoulder girdle.*

Lying on your stomach, your arms extended in front of you and your thumbs pointed toward the ceiling, lift your arms off the floor by pinching your shoulder blades together. Keep your head on the floor and don't arch your lower back. Lift and hold for a couple seconds, lower, and repeat ten times.

Plank *Promotes core strength.*

Get onto your hands and knees, as though you are about to begin a push up, then extend your legs behind you, tucking your toes under your feet, so that your body forms a straight line from your head to your feet. Keep your arms straight and in line with your shoulders. Use your abdominal muscles to hold your body in alignment. Hold for thirty seconds to a minute, rest, and repeat. You can also do this pose with your arms bent, keeping your elbows under your shoulders and your forearms pointed straight ahead, parallel to one another.

Side Plank   *Promotes core strength.*

Begin on your side, resting on one elbow, your legs stacked and aligned with your torso. Engaging your abdominal muscles, press up with your grounded forearm, and lift your hips until your legs and torso form a straight line. Hold for thirty seconds to a minute and switch sides. Repeat two times on each side.

Hamstring Stretch

What we know as the hamstring is actually a group of muscles running along the back of the thigh. The hamstrings are employed in most types of physical activity, so it's not that surprising that tight hamstrings are common in active people.

To work on loosening tight hamstrings, begin on your back with your feet flat on the floor. Straighten one leg and wrap a rolled towel or yoga strap around the arch of the foot of the other. Keeping your back on the floor, extend the leg toward the ceiling, straightening the leg to the extent you are able to do so. Keeping your leg as straight as possible, use the strap or towel to pull your leg toward your head. Don't worry about how far you are able to pull the leg toward you. Rather, focus on keeping your leg straight, your hips square, and your back on the floor. Hold for thirty seconds, then switch legs. Repeat four times, or for a total of two minutes on each side.

Iliotilial (IT) Band Stretch

The IT band runs down the side of the thigh from the side of the hip to just below the knee. Tightness of the IT band and associated muscles can lead to improper alignment, muscle imbalances and pain. This IT band stretch will help to loosen the IT band, the hips and surrounding muscles.

It's good to do this stretch as a follow-up to the lying down hamstring stretch, as you'll already be in the right position. If you're starting fresh, lie on your back and straighten one leg on the floor as you bend the other toward your chest, wrapping a rolled towel or yoga strap around the arch of your foot. Next, extend the leg toward the ceiling, keeping it straight. Now rotate the hip of the extended leg out at a 45-degree angle and pull the strap and your leg across your body until you feel a pull in the hip of the working leg. Keep your back on the floor. Hold this position for thirty seconds, release and switch legs. Repeat four times, or for a total of two minutes on each leg.

Quadricep Stretch

The quadriceps are the large muscles running along the front and sides of the thigh. Begin standing tall, with your feet facing forward. Bend one leg behind you, clasping your ankle or the top of your foot in your hand. Pull the foot toward your butt, pointing your knee straight toward the floor, and pushing your hip slightly forward. Hold for thirty seconds, switch legs, and repeat four times on each leg or until you reach two minutes on each leg. If you have trouble balancing, hold onto a wall or a railing with your free hand.

Calf Stretch

The calf muscles are those running between the knee and the ankle at the back of the leg. For a simple stretch you can do almost anywhere, stand a foot or so from a wall. Bring one foot back far enough to bend your other leg into a very shallow lunge. Pitch your torso forward, placing your hands against the wall. Keep both feet pointed straight ahead as you do this and aim to keep your back leg straight and your heel pressed toward the floor. Hold for thirty seconds, switch sides, and repeat four times on each leg or until you reach two minutes on each side.

Ulnar Nerve Stretch

Bicyclists commonly experience numbness or tingling in the palms of the hand related to gripping or leaning on handlebars for extended periods of time. This stretch can help to remedy and prevent this sensation. Stand up straight, and bring the palms of your hands up to your cheekbones, your fingers facing behind you. Pinching your shoulder blades together, flex your elbows backward until you feel a stretch along the underside of your forearms and an opening across the chest. Now bring your elbows back toward one another with your hands remaining in place and repeat this opening and closing motion slowly twenty times.

Cycle Style Around The Globe:
The Growing Fashionability of the Humble Bicycle

"You know how they say don't judge a book by her cover? I think you can…(W)hen we dress, it's expressing who we are. I think it's fabulous."
-Catherine Baba, Paris fashion icon, stylist, and bike commuter[50]

"It was not a question of knowledge . . . but of alertness, a fastidious transcription of what could be thought about something, once it swam into the stream of attention."
-Susan Sontag[51]

When I spent a college semester in Paris in the early 2000s, I was mesmerized by the beauty of the place: the buildings dripping in architectural detail and history, the delicious, yeast-filled smells of my neighborhood courtesy of the corner boulangerie, the sunny plazas where Parisians spent languid afternoons relaxing, canoodling, and chattering away in their mellifluous, lilting language in a haze of cigarette smoke. These were people who seemed born into sophistication and who looked as though they could have danced off the pages of a fashion magazine.

I returned to Paris in 2014 for the first time in more than a decade to find it mostly as I remembered it, with two very striking exceptions: smoking had been banished from a surprising number of public spaces and bicycles were everywhere. The City of Lights, if you'll excuse the pun, had in my absence become a city of bikes.

It wasn't strapping, spandex-clad road warriors that caught my eye in this, the land of the Tour de France. Rather, it was the urban bicycling crowd, comprising perfectly put-together men and women who pedaled past me in cool three-quarter length coats cinched about their waists, carrying dogs or yoga mats, baguettes or briefcases in their baskets. They wore ballet flats, boots, and stylish tennis shoes and scarves draped cooly around their necks in a technique I've never been able to perfect.

Unlike most of the camera-toting tourists milling about the streets in this most-visited place in the world, snapping photos of Notre Dame and the Louvre, my camera lens was perpetually tuned to the effortlessly chic women pedaling past. It didn't take long for my traveling companion to tire of my bordering-on-obsessive photographic scavenger hunt, and we soon agreed upon a compromise wherein I would, reluctantly, leave my camera at our rental apartment at certain times of day.

Over my semester in Paris in the early 2000s, I can't even remember seeing a bike. I'm sure there were a few, but I'm also quite certain that if bicycles had been any significant component of the Parisian cityscape, I most definitely would have returned to the U.S. with an urban bicycling habit to complement the monochromatic wardrobe, affinity for strong cheeses, and slightest hint of a French accent picked up on my adventures abroad.

The rise of urban biking in Paris is largely credited to the arrival in 2007 of Vélib', the city's bike share system that is now one of the largest in the world, with more than 20,000 bikes set up at kiosks around the city.[52] In the saddles of the chunky, metallic colored rent-a-bikes and on bikes of their own, Parisians are taking to the bike en masse.

In the first five years after the introduction of bike share in Paris, the number of trips taken by bike increased 41 percent to an estimated three percent of all trips.[53] As of 2015, the overall bicycle share of trips had risen to around five percent. As many as 150,000 Vélib' trips are made daily, according to the company that runs the system.[54] City officials boast that more than one Vélib' bike is rented every second.[55] Another 200,000 trips or so are taken on privately owned bikes in Paris daily.[56]

Paris, of course, isn't exceptional in its embrace of the bicycle, particularly in Europe, which has long excelled in promoting alternatives to the automobile. But that the world's fashion capital has hopped into the saddle to such an extent is, to my mind, quite remarkable. To say that style and biking have not always been regarded as complementary ideals is putting it mildly. And yet Paris is one of the cities proving just how very fashionable the bike can be.

"The bicycle is increasingly part of the vocabulary of street style," says Brent Luvaas, an associate professor of visual anthropology at Drexel University in Philadelphia. Luvaas, the photographer behind the blog Urban Field Notes (www.urbanfieldnotes.com) and the author of the book *Street Style: An Ethnography of Fashion Blogging*, studies street style and street style blogs as a means of documenting larger cultural and social changes through clothing. "People are seeing bikes very much as fashion accessories, not just modes of transport," Luvaas says, adding that this is especially true among certain urban subsets of the population.

The fashion and marketing worlds are paying attention. Today, the bicycle can be found on billboards, beers labels, and banking ads. It serves as the backdrop for trendy mobile food businesses, is featured as "must-have" accessories in the glossy pages of fashion magazines, and appears in the Style section of the *New York Times*.

"Roadways are the new runways," that publication declared a few years back in a piece examining the proliferation of style-conscious female cyclists in the Big Apple.[57] Even the Catholic Church (admittedly not an institution one would describe as being on the forefront of the latest trends) is getting on the bike bandwagon. "Pope Francis revealed that it pains him when he sees a nun or priest driving an expensive car," reporter Carol Glatz wrote in 2013, "and he praised the beauty of the bicycle, noting his 54-year-old personal secretary, Msgr Alfred Xuereb, gets around on a bike." [58]

In some cases, the appropriation of the bike as marketing tool comes with unintended hilarity. The mall near my city used a smiling, attractive couple pedaling around on bike to advertise its spring shopping push this year, never mind the fact that it's all but impossible to bike anywhere near this monument to suburban sprawl. Haute couturier Hermes, best known for its fancy scarves and Birkin bags that retail for tens of thousands of dollars, has decided to tap in to the fashionability of bikes in a more direct way with a line of handmaid bicycles that fetch around $11,000 each.[59]

From well-known companies like Levi's to plucky upstart brands like Brooklyn-based Outlier, clothing manufacturers are jumping into the fray to create functional—and fashionable—clothing and gear designed expressly with the bicycle commuter in mind. And while the bicycling industry hasn't traditionally done a great job of catering to women's needs, increasingly, the clothing and bicycling industries are acknowledging the existence and value of the female bicycling market.

Simultaneously, fashions in some quarters appear to be trending toward a more relaxed style. Sweats and tennis shoes once relegated to lazy weekends around the house or sweating away at the gym are getting a pricey makeover, sold for top dollar by a growing sweep of clothing companies seeking to tap the market for what the research and marketing firms have dubbed "athleisure." Call it the Lululemon effect: Increasingly, it seems, consumers, and especially millennial women, are in search of clothes that transition from the gym to the office to a night on the town.[60]

Experts note that it's not necessarily a change in urban activity levels that are stoking this shift. (After all, fashion is not always rooted in practical considerations.) Even so, it seems noteworthy that this evolution of the American fashion landscape would coincide with a transformation of the transportation landscape.

Some observers wonder whether the bicycle might actually be helping to change fashions, just as it did at the dawn of the 20th century.

"I notice it in small ways around Philadelphia," says Luvaas, who says he sees quite a few men and women walking around with their right pants leg rolled right up, that telltale sign of bicycle ridership. He also notes a growing affinity for low-maintenance hairstyles that look purposefully disheveled (and might recover more readily from the effects of the helmet) in certain creative industries and academia, historically home to strong bicycling ranks.

Luvaas thinks fashion may even help to explain the American gender disparity in bicycling. Men's garments tend to lend themselves more readily to the activity, he says. Moreover, the bicycle may simply be associated in the public consciousness with a male, urban subculture that many women don't relate to.

The upside? Fashions can change.

"There is no biological reason that men would bike more than women," says Luvaas. "It's simply about norms that have been in circulation for a long time." Luvaas was covering New York Fashion Week in September, 2014 when model-blogger-photographer and street style star Hanneli Mustaparta showed up on a bicycle, causing quite a stir among the crowd. (In a *Vogue* article, Mustaparta described the bike as a favored mode of transportation and demonstrated the feasibility of wearing heels on a bicycle, though she conceded she sometimes bikes barefoot and carries her heels in her basket.[61]) To Luvaas' mind, Mustaparta was making a very conscious fashion choice.

Pedal Chic is a woman-oriented bike shop opened in Greenville, South Carolina that sells everything from sleek racing bikes and jerseys to commuter bikes and active wear. The shop feels more

like a boutique than a bike shop, with its drapes, mannequins, and aromatherapy ("I didn't want it to smell like rubber tires," owner Robin Bylenga explains). There's even a runway set up at the center of the store.

Bylenga found her way to the bike business after being downsized from a corporate job, going to work for another bike shop, and realizing a need for a store that created a community for women of all bicycling experience levels and interests.

Greenville has a long tradition of road cycling. It is the home of George Hincapie, the retired professional cyclist who rode alongside Lance Armstrong in his seven (since revoked, post-doping revelations) Tour de France victories, and hosts a number of well-known cycling races and training events.

But with increasing frequency, amid lots of downtown investment and the idea of walkable and bikeable living gaining currency in Greenville as it is elsewhere in the U.S., Bylenga notices a different type of customer coming into her shop: women who don't necessarily define themselves as cyclists who come in search of functional and fashionable apparel and accessories for urban biking. These are items like racks, strong locks, high-tech, water-wicking fabrics fashioned into stylish dresses and commuter jeans, a brand of chamois underwear that flies of the shelves, and $250 rain capes.

"Our market," she says, "is changing."

A recent analysis by the U.S. Census Bureau found that bike commuting is most common among the most and least educated Americans and those that fall on the highest and lowest extremes of the household income scale, more than likely capturing those who have little alternative on the one end and those who do so by choice on the other.[62]

African Americans, Asians, and Hispanics are leading growth in bicycling. In the U.S. African American bicycle trips rose 100 percent between 2001 and 2009, compared with just 22 percent among whites.[63] But at 0.3 percent, black workers had a lower rate of bike commuting than any other racial group.[64] Statistics show that a higher proportion of African Americans are unemployed, which could help to explain the disparity since journey-to-work figures don't account for the non-working public. As of April 2015, the seasonally adjusted unemployment rate for African Americans stood at 9.6 percent, more than double that of the white population.[65] Notably, the rate of unemployment among women of all races age twenty and over was 8.8 percent—double that of men in the same age range.

At the same time that many white, more affluent Americans want to drive less, it seems that many poor Americans still see the car as a sign of financial and social success. So concluded researchers Eve

Bratman and Adam Jadhav based on surveys conducted in Washington, D.C. in 2012 and 2013 that found African Americans were statistically more likely than other groups to desire automobiles.[66] "Automobility remains a paradoxical cultural and status symbol," they wrote, "such that while wealthier people increasingly reduce their car dependency, poor people still aspire to car ownership."[67]

"There's this association that a lot of us still have where people without other options ride a bike," says Luvaas of this phenomenon. White, middle and upper class people have the luxury of not needing automobiles to demonstrate that they've "made it."

Veronica Davis, a civil engineer living in Washington, D.C., co-founded the group Black Women Bike in 2011 with the aim of introducing more women to the possibility of biking.

Davis started biking for transportation in 2009 amid rising gas prices and the launch of a new business that had her looking to cut costs wherever possible. In 2011, she was pedaling past a public housing complex when she heard a little black girl exclaim, "Mommy, mommy, mommy, there's a black lady on a bike!" It was as though the girl had just spotted Michelle Obama, Davis told the crowd at the National Bike Summit in 2013.[68] She realized that she was the first person on a bike the little girl had seen who looked like her.

It was a powerful moment that inspired the launch of Black Women Bike, which started as a Facebook group (now 1,500 members strong) and has given rise to regular programming that includes group rides and workshops that teach participants skills ranging from how to ride in the street to how to fix a flat.

Davis says black women are held back from bicycling by a wide range of obstacles, but prominent among them is the simple fact that they don't see many other women who look like them pedaling around in the bike lane—or in the media. It's important, she says, to combat the notion that you need to be white, young, and a size two to ride a bike.

"We need to see more images of women who represent the true diversity of cyclists, not just racially but also age and size-wise," Davis says. "If you can get one black woman on a bike, you can get three," she adds. "People don't want to ride alone."

Meantime, back in Paris, the world's fashion capital has recently announced its aims to reinvent itself as a global cycling capital.

In 2015, amid mounting concerns about the severe air pollution problems that have crippled the city in recent years, the Parisian government unveiled a grand, five-year plan intended to increase its cycling ranks. As part of this effort, city officials proposed $164 million in bike-related investments that they hope will triple the share of trips made by bike to 15 percent by 2020. This would be accomplished in part by doubling the city's bike lane network to 870 miles, funding stipends to offset the cost of buying bicycles, installing thousands of new bike parking facilities, and lowering speed limits on certain roads.[69]

Paris has also been working to bring new age groups into the cycling mix. In 2014, Vélib' expanded to children through a program called, adorably, P'tit Vélib', with three-hundred child-sized bikes added to stations across the city in an effort to get kids developing healthy, eco-friendly transportation habits early on.[70] The city is also considering adding an electric bike component to its bike share program to help those who need some extra assistance getting around.

Outfitting Your Ride

You Don't Have to Wear Spandex to Ride a Bike (But You Can if You Want To)

In many countries, bicycling wear is everyday wear, and this idea is quickly gaining currency in the U.S. There are a growing number of clothing companies catching on to the market for fashion-conscious urban bicyclists. They are tweaking staples like jeans, dresses, and jackets with novelties such as reflective details, anti-microbial fabrics, and reinforced crotches to better withstand the extra stress of the saddle. Yet while some of these new lines are filling an important gap in the marketplace (the pricey pair of tight black bike-commuter pants I purchased recently and tend to wear even on days I don't ride my bike have helped to make me a believer), the reality is that you don't need a new wardrobe to ride your bike.

The Best Clothes for Biking

You can wear just about anything on a bike, though some articles of clothing work better than others. I generally avoid long skirts, which can get snagged in the chain, and stick to pants with a tapered leg or those with legs that are easily rolled to mid-calf for the same reason. Skinny jeans can work great on a bike, unless they're too tight to comfortably bend your legs or are so low-cut in the back that they show off more than you intended. Leggings or tights and flowy tops are among my bicycling go-to's, though women who are more substantially endowed than I may find that too-flowy tops reveal a little more than they intended as they're bent over handlebars. In the summer months, I'll work shorts and even some shorter dresses and skirts into the mix.

In terms of footwear, I generally stick to flats, though this tends to be the case no matter my mode of transportation. Flexible ballet flats work great for me on a bike, as they do in most other settings, while other, more rigid shoe types have given me some pretty horrendous blisters. If you're ardent about elevation, platform wedges have served me well on my bike, though I know some women cyclists swear by the irregular sole geometry afforded by heels in helping to keep one's foot properly-positioned on the pedal.

Accessorize to Make Your Commute More Comfortable & Safe

GLOVES

In winter, gloves' advantages are obvious. But even in hot weather, a pair of basic fingerless cycling gloves readily available at the closest bike shop can help you maintain your grip on the handlebars, which tend to become slippery with sweat. They can also help to keep your hands from getting sore and stave off numbness if you've got an especially lengthy commute. In this latter instance, gloves with a little more padding can help to ease any hand discomfort.

How to make your skirt FLASH-FREE

I was introduced recently to an elegantly simple technique for making even a short skirt bike friendly. To perform the skirt-cinching method a group of British women in a popular online video dubbed "Penny in Yo' Pants," one only needs a penny or some other coin denomination and a rubber band or hair tie, though I'd guess even a string would work. Push the penny against the fabric from the back of your skirt through your legs, grabbing back and front fabric layers together. Next, loop the rubber band around the fabric-bundled coin until it is secured into a button. You can view the video instruction at pennyinyourpants.co.uk.

My friend Christina recommends the Monica glove by Giro. These heavily-padded gloves are made for distance, are tailored for women, and retail for around $40. If you're simply looking to improve your grip for warm-weather riding conditions, you might try a pair of gloves with a vented mesh back.

PANNIERS

If your load is light and the temperatures are mild, a backpack or messenger bag may be all you need. But trust me: panniers, also known as saddle bags, which hook to or drape over the carrying rack on your bike, will change your life by making it vastly more comfortable to get around by bike while carrying the things that you need. Panniers come in all variety of shapes, sizes, and materials to suit your tastes and load. Over time, you might invest in several types to best accommodate what you want to carry on your bike. I, for one, have a pannier that I use when I have my laptop in tow that is waterproof and insulated; a set of open-top panniers made for carrying bags of groceries that also work great for everyday riding purposes; another, commodious set of the roll-top, waterproof variety that I use when I have a good bit to carry and the weather looks threatening; and a small and stylish bag that hooks to my rack or to the front of my bike and doubles as a cross-body purse or clutch for going out. I have met up with friends for a meal or drinks many times with my bulky, square panniers slung over my shoulder, but it can be a challenge keeping them out of the way of anyone or anything.

LIGHTS

Lights or reflectors are required by cyclists in all states after dark. I like to ride with lights on even during the day, especially early in the morning and when the light starts to fade in the evening. Invest in a high-quality set of front and rear bike lights (white in the front and red in the rear) and use them religiously. A good front light is not only essential for avoiding obstructions in the streets after dark; it's also important for helping drivers, other cyclists, and pedestrians see you.

FENDERS

I never appreciated the value of fenders until I started riding to work regularly without them. In my pre-fender days, riding through even a small puddle would leave my back and calves splattered with droplets of water and mud, making me look like I'd pedaled through an obstacle course. Today, thanks to these simple metal strips, I can handle even post-storm roads without the splatter effect. Bikes that don't come equipped with fenders can usually be outfitted with a pair fairly inexpensively.

A CHAINGUARD

Chainguards that come standard on many city bikes provide a barrier between the chain and your pants leg. They not only help to prevent damage to clothes but also the potentially dangerous situation that can occur when the fabric gets stuck in the chain, which in some cases can cause a rider to topple over. If you don't have a chainguard and are wearing pants, you can roll your right pant leg before riding, or invest in a simple strap that holds the fabric tight against your leg. Wearing pants that are tapered around calf and ankle can also help to minimize the chances of getting your clothing stuck in the chain or dirty.

A REARVIEW MIRROR

Bike mirrors can be picked up for a few dollars at the bike shop, be attached to either your helmet or handlebars, and can make it much easier to detect what's going on behind you.

A HELMET

The helmet is exactly no one's favorite cycling accessory. And if the only interest that mattered were style, my helmet would get left behind every time I rode my bike. In New Orleans, and many other cities, there are no laws requiring helmets for adult cyclists. Consequently, I find that my helmet-wearing habit places me in the distinct minority among everyday riders. As I pedal around the city, my head dutifully covered, I sometimes feel like a geeky prude among all the un-helmeted cyclists whizzing by, their free-flowing manes evoking in me the occasional twinge of envy. Then I think of some of the people I know who credit their lives (or at least sustained brain function) to wearing a helmet—among them are my brother, my husband, and several dear friends—and I quickly get over it.

These days, manufacturers are helping to make helmet-wearing much more stylish. There are urban helmets that forgo the not-so-subtle venting systems and aerodynamic irregularity of their recreational counterparts in favor of a sleeker, more streamlined and modern aesthetic. A few companies even make helmets designed to be worn under interchangeable hats that render them barely distinguishable from a fashionable fedora. Meantime, a pair of women in Sweden have come up with an invisible "helmet" that is worn as a collar around the neck and deploys on impact, much like the airbag on a car.

Selecting a Helmet

Pulling one of those circa-1980 egg-shaped domes out of your shed probably won't give you the kind of protection you need. Helmets deteriorate over time, even if they haven't been involved in a crash (in which case it's definitely time to trade your helmet in for a new model). In selecting a helmet, you'll find lots of variety in style, shape, and price. Bicycle helmets can run anywhere from $20 up to a few hundred. But unless you're looking for specific racing performance or aesthetic characteristics, it doesn't matter much how much you spend. Whether you buy your helmet at the bike shop down the street or at your local big box store, it's required to meet federal safety standards. Look for the Consumer Product Safety Commission decal, which lets you know it's compliant.

Your helmet should fit snuggly on the top of your head, cover much of your forehead, and be tight enough so that it's not able to slide around. The strap should be adjusted so that the helmet fits snugly and no more than two fingers fit between the strap and your chin.

When you're on your bike, there's no such thing as standing out too much. Bright-colored, white, or reflective clothing and accessories can make you far more visible to drivers and other cyclists, especially when riding at night, early morning, at dusk, or in rainy weather. This doesn't mean your wardrobe has to look like it comes straight from the disco era. If your style tends toward the muted side of the spectrum and you prefer to keep it that way, simply toss some colorful or reflective accessories into your bag that you can wear as needed. Ideas for accessories that don't take up a ton of space include: a reflective vest or jacket; a neon or light-up scarf; strips of velcro reflective material that you can strap to your arms and legs; and decals that adhere to helmets, bags and your body. Some bag manufacturers make neon reflective models that work like a charm for bicycling. I've even seen reflective and glow-in-the-dark helmets that can help get you noticed when it counts. You can also purchase iron-on reflective tape for a few dollars. Attach it in a strip inside the back of the leg opening of your favorite jeans, flip up the cuffs when you ride and—voila—you've got a killer pair of pants for your bike commute.

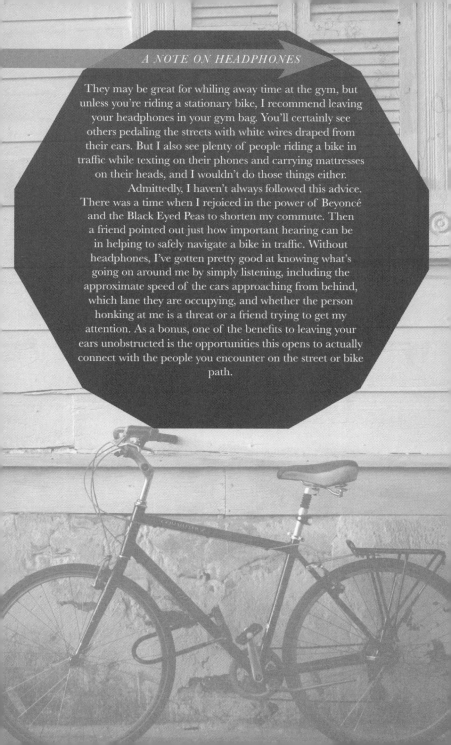

A NOTE ON HEADPHONES

They may be great for whiling away time at the gym, but unless you're riding a stationary bike, I recommend leaving your headphones in your gym bag. You'll certainly see others pedaling the streets with white wires draped from their ears. But I also see plenty of people riding a bike in traffic while texting on their phones and carrying mattresses on their heads, and I wouldn't do those things either.

Admittedly, I haven't always followed this advice. There was a time when I rejoiced in the power of Beyoncé and the Black Eyed Peas to shorten my commute. Then a friend pointed out just how important hearing can be in helping to safely navigate a bike in traffic. Without headphones, I've gotten pretty good at knowing what's going on around me by simply listening, including the approximate speed of the cars approaching from behind, which lane they are occupying, and whether the person honking at me is a threat or a friend trying to get my attention. As a bonus, one of the benefits to leaving your ears unobstructed is the opportunities this opens to actually connect with the people you encounter on the street or bike path.

Women at Work

"Riding my bike to work actually gave me some cool points. Most people at the office seemed impressed or interested in it, and I quickly became "the bike chick," in a good way. It's been a part of my work identity for a few years."
-Christine Moser, New Orleans architect and bike commuter

I believe that the opinions of your boss and coworkers can have lots of influence over your willingness to ride. I know of workplaces that encourage their employees to travel by alternative means by offering showers, lockers, transit passes, and rebates for not taking up expensive parking spaces. On the other hand, I've heard of offices that exhibit real hostility to the practice, whether overt or less direct.

I've also noticed that one person can make a big difference in shaping the culture of an office. A friend of mine started out as the lone bike commuter at a small design firm a few years ago. Today his workplace is populated by a band of ardent bike commuters.

There's some solid research out there suggesting that this contagious effect is found not just on the level of the workplace, but also in neighborhoods, friend circles, and even across entire cities.[71] To me, it serves as an inspiring reminder of the importance of even one person's actions in helping to set the tone of a place and make real change.

Being the only person in the office who bicycles to work can be an intimidating experience, but some find real reward—and even accolades—in operating outside the norm. "It felt good to be contributing to changing perceptions, making it a new norm," said Sarah Hammitt, an urban planner now living in New Jersey who used to bike to work at New Orleans City Hall. "When I biked to work, I was praised more than anything," said Lauren Bordelon, a librarian who was one of three bike commuters at the elementary school where she used to work in Norman, Oklahoma. "My kids loved when my bike was parked in the library," she added. "It was like I had brought the best show and tell ever."

Of course, it's not just feeling like an outsider that holds women back from biking to the office. Starting in 2012, I conducted a four-month survey about challenges and incentives to biking for transportation in New Orleans. The survey wasn't randomized, but as it happened, the majority of the 807 surveys completed were completed by working women who had access to at least one car and typically drove to work.

Survey takers were asked to rank how a number of enumerated obstacles—factors including concerns about safety, weather, and roads—played into their transportation decisions. They were also able to write in concerns of their own. A theme quickly emerged from the write-in responses that I naively hadn't thought to include in my multiple-choice selections. From worries over "helmet hair," to arriving sweaty to a meeting, to one attorney who fretted over wrinkling her suit en route to the office, women respondents not infrequently said they were kept out of the saddle by their worries about the bicycle's effect on their appearance.

Much has been made of the scrutiny applied to women's appearance in the workplace and beyond. As Stanford law professor Deborah Rhode, author of *The Beauty Bias: The Injustice of Appearance in Life and Law*, told the *New York Times*, "The quality of my teaching shouldn't depend on the color of my lipstick or whether I've got mascara on."[72] Yet researchers have found a link between women's body weight and workplace earnings and status, with no similar connection identified among men.[73] Another study found that women who wore makeup were perceived as more competent, likeable, and trustworthy. (That study, it should be noted, was funded by Proctor & Gamble, which manufactures Covergirl cosmetics, among other similar products.)[74]

I'm by no means suggesting that women are the only ones who face pressure to look good; I think it's safe to say, however, that the bar for men isn't set quite as high.

One of the first things I noticed about my co-workers the last time I started a new job was just how put together everyone was. The women in their heels and pencil skirts and men in their crisp shirts and neckties stood in stark contrast to the T-shirts and holey jeans that were standard at my university job, where the only neckties on display were those worn ironically. And whereas I had been accustomed to arriving at my old job to find the bike rack closest to my office filled to capacity, mine was typically the lone bicycle parked at the shiny architectural bike rack outside my new workplace.

As I explored my new surroundings on my first day at work (I drove, wanting to be sure I arrived looking as manicured as possible), I casually inquired as a co-worker took me on a tour about the showers I'd heard about through a friend of a friend. Their presence had been near the top of the list of perks I'd pointed out to others in enumerating the virtues of my new job.

My tour guide showed me to the shower stall tucked behind the lavatory in the backroom, advising that I be discreet about using it. It was a subtle indication I took to mean that that those in charge were less than enthusiastic about employees bicycling to work. I was crestfallen, and a little worried about what I had signed up for.

Part of me wondered if I should just suck it up and drive to the office. After all, at least I had a job in a market in which many of my friends were still looking for work. Was biking to work really worth the prospective alienation? But in thinking it over that night, I decided that there was nothing frivolous about my decision to get to work by bike. As long as I was showing up to work on time, how I got there was really nobody's business. I would prove, I determined, that biking to work was not only feasible, but that I could do it without looking like a slob.

I went online that night and bought a couple of pairs of office-appropriate pants made of fast-drying, sweat-wicking material from one of the growing array of stores that make fashionable athletic wear designed for the gym and beyond. Later that week, I biked to work for the first time, a little nervous and self-conscious, but also invigorated by the experience.

My hesitation about biking to work has given way to an unmitigated sense of pride about the practice—and far less guilt about indulging in one of the donuts that perennially appear in the office break room. I've also learned that I'm not alone in my bike-riding interest. Some days, I arrive to work to find two or three other bikes already tethered outside to the bike rack. This past Bike to Work Day saw quadruple the participation of the previous year at our office, and in the break room, I occasionally overhear conversations about the benefits of biking to the office from some of the very the people I was most worried about not understanding my interest in it. I'm determined that one day, I'll even get my boss to give biking to work a try.

How to Look Presentable After Biking to Work, Even Without a Shower

I'm heartened in knowing that the more people who take to two wheels, the more normalized the practice will become and the less offensive a little bit of sweat will seem. It is quite possible, however, to bicycle to work without abandoning all hopes of looking office-appropriate. I can think of several women off the top of my head who manage to bicycle to work most days of the week and look as presentable, professional, and competent as anyone else.

If your work does not offer bicycle parking, then a nearby street sign, pole or fence may suffice as a safe place to lock up instead. Refer to page 115 for more details.

"I don't get any sweatier biking somewhere than I would walking or taking the bus," said Tara Tolford, a regular New Orleans bike commuter whom I count in this number. "There's very little exertion involved in everyday cycling for short distances. I can bike in anything I'd wear otherwise except pencil skirts. The only thing that gives me grief, appearance-wise, is that helmets are hot and make your hair sweaty and gross, so pulled-back is basically the only option."

Despite my initial excitement over the shower at my office, I still haven't used it. I haven't polled my coworkers, but after ten minutes spent freshening up in the restroom post-ride, I don't feel as though I am readily distinguishable from those who drove to work, except I probably look a little happier and more alert.

I like to shower at home before getting on my bike. After I arrive at the office, I'll dry off a bit. Those paper toilet seat covers found in many public restrooms work like a charm for sopping up sweat, and they're also great for freshening up your makeup during the day. (Like those expensive blotting papers that you might find at the makeup counter, they remove oils that cause shine.) Next, I swipe a cleansing cloth over my face and body, re-apply deodorant, brush my hair back into a neat ponytail and—if it's an especially hot day and I'm worried about my scent—spritz myself with the body spray I keep on-hand at the office. I don't wear a ton of makeup, but what I do wear, I usually hold off on applying until this point, especially when it's hot out, so that it's not streaked across my face upon my arrival. All of the essentials I need—body wipes, makeup, brush and deodorant—fit into a plastic makeup bag I carry with me on my bike. If there's storage space, you might even try leaving a few of these items at the office.

GETTING YOUR HAIR WORK-READY IN A PINCH

Hair has never been one of my strong suits. Despite my best intentions, I never make it back to the salon for cuts at anything close to the recommended schedule. I rejoiced in learning of the ombre trend, which just so happened to align with my own accidental, root-exposed style that is the result of too-infrequent trips to the colorist for highlights. My go-to treatment for work typically involves little more effort than pulling my sometimes-still-damp dirty-blond locks back into a bun or ponytail. A dressier occasion usually demands running a straightening iron through my hair, one of the few styling techniques I can safely say that I've mastered. And I long ago resigned myself to the fact that on days that I bike to the office, my hair is going to be a lost cause.

Then, on one of my rare trips to the salon for a haircut, I met Chris Kijko. Kijko, a native of England who currently resides in New Orleans, is not just a hair stylist extraordinaire. He's also a competitive cyclist. This being a combination I have not frequently encountered, I took advantage of the opportunity to attempt to improve my hair game.

"One of the key elements to any hair styling is to start with accepting your hair's natural texture," Kijko advises. "Any time you work with exactly what your hair does naturally, you'll have a much easier time and a better result."

This is all-the-more-true for women who bike, Kijko says, and it is especially so for women who bicycle in humid locales like New Orleans. That's because any time your hair gets even a little bit wet, no amount of product and preparation will save it from reverting back to what nature intended. You can spend hours straightening the waves out of your curly hair first thing in the morning. But once you expose it to sweat and humidity, Kijko says, "you're basically going to be starting fresh."

His advice: work with what you've got. Figure out how your hair behaves without any intervention at all and you'll be able to come up with some strategies for accentuating its inherent beauty.

African American hair has lots of texture to it, posing a significant challenge for any would-be black woman bicyclist who wants to keep her hair stick straight. Kijko is heartened by the recent trend among some black women toward embracing their hair's natural state. Not only can African American hair prove stunning when worn in this way, Kijko says; it also stands a much better chance of holding up to the elements.

Veronica Davis of Black Women Bike, meantime, offers up a simple tip for staving off helmet hair that she says has proven effective for women of all races and hair types: "Wear a satin scarf under your helmet," she advises. "Tie it on your head." Davis says the satin protects against rubbing, keeps hair in place, and helps to absorb sweat. "It has to be satin," she says. "Cotton will cling."

Try this test:

Next time you wash your hair, let it air dry, then spend some time scrutinizing yourself in the mirror. Are you one of the rare few whose hair is naturally silky and smooth? Is your mane a mass of tightly-wound ringlets? Or are your locks (like mine) somewhere in between, an untamed cataclysm of curly cues and straight lines sticking every which way?

If your hair is naturally straight, shiny and smooth, it probably won't need much post-ride fixing. Flatness may be a concern, Kijko says, but styling your hair could be as simple as running a brush through it and teasing it out a bit once it's dry. For those of us who fall on the opposite end of the hair texture spectrum, however, a few extra steps taken upon arrival at the office may be all that's required to feel appropriately put together.

If your hair has natural wave to it and you don't feel like pulling it back into an updo, a curling iron stashed at the workplace can work wonders in very little time, Kijko says. If your hair is sweaty, you'll want to dry it out first, or let it air dry. (If you don't have a hair dryer at the office, you could even try one of those hand dryers found in many commercial bathrooms. The aim is not smoothing your hair with the dryer, but simply getting the dampness out of it.) Next, twist the curling iron around several sections of your hair, just enough so that you've provided some "organization" to your natural waves. "Because it doesn't have to be super organized, it can be made really pretty really easily," Kijko advises.

What's In My Bike Bag

The primary bag I use for biking to work and around town looks like many women's purses. It is an abyss of old receipts, wadded-up napkins, and way too many tubes of chapstick. But it's also filled with some pretty useful stuff, including my driver's license and insurance card; transit fare (in case my bike breaks down and I can't easily fix it); a credit card; a bike lock; a multi-purpose tool with Allen and crescent wrenches for tightening loose components, removing wheels and other on-the-go maintenance needs; a set of tire levers; a spare tube; a rubber glove to keep my hands from getting too greasy if I need to fix a flat; a patch kit and a hand pump. Most of these items I never touch on a day-to-day basis. But on the occasions that I've needed them, they have proven indispensable.

When I'm commuting to work, I'll throw in some extras: A quick-drying cloth or cleansing wipes; a plastic baggie to keep my phone dry if it rains; a rain jacket or poncho; my makeup bag; a change of clothes; and an energy bar for when my stomach starts grumbling mid-morning.

....

1. A rubber glove (to keep grease off at least one of my hands should I need to make a repair).

2. A tool kit case (which typically houses: *10.* a multitool; *7.* puncture repair patches; *8.* a pair of tire levers; and *13.* a spare tube)

3. My makeup bag (with deodorant, moisturizer, a few key cosmetic items and brushes, and a disposable cleansing cloth.)

4. A brush   *5.* A hair tie   *6.* My u-lock

9. A large wrench (This is overkill in light of the multitool, which contains several variety of wrenches, but I find the leverage provided by this full-size version makes it much easier for me to use it.)

11. An extra flashing light   *12.* A hand pump   *14.* Chapstick and lip gloss

15. My cell phone (protected in a ziplock bag in case of rain)

16. A super-absorbant, fast-drying towel

17. A bicycle saddle cover (for use after locking up my bike outside when it looks like rain)

18. Transit fare

19. My driver's license and (again overkill in light of the cash) a transit fare card

20. My credit and health insurance cards

Can you get by with far less than this and do just fine?
Absolutely. But I find some comfort in being over-prepared.

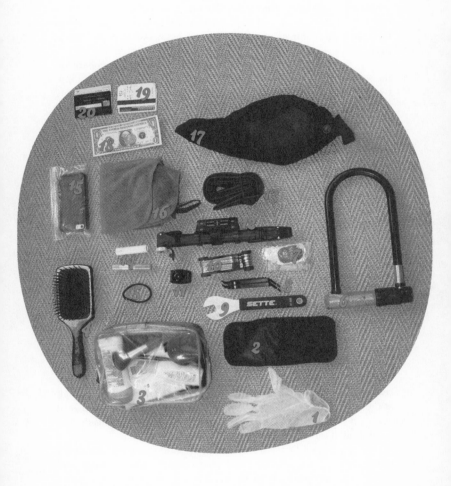

What to Wear to Bike to Work

To my earlier assertion that you can wear almost anything you want to ride a bike, I'll add this caveat: It's not always easy to find the right thing to wear to bike to work. It's one thing to show up to meet friends for brunch on a Saturday morning looking sweaty and disheveled; it's another to show up to greet your suited-up boss, clients, or coworkers that way. (There are, of course, places in which so many people bike to the office where this stigma against sweatiness is overcome by critical mass.)

My own bike-commute wardrobe is highly dependent on the seasons, which in South Louisiana can essentially be divided into two: pleasant and sweltering. While some look forward to the onset of football, pumpkin latte and boots season, for me, among the foremost perks of fall is the break from oppressive summer heat and humidity. This is prime bike-to-work season. It means I can ride my bike to the office without looking like a drowned rat upon my arrival, and that I can usually make the commute without worrying with a change of clothes. A bike-friendly, work-appropriate wardrobe is mostly dependent on fabric, style, and the art of layering, all dependent on the weather.

RIDING IN THE HEAT

In milder weather, my bike-commute staples are a pair of tapered-leg pants and a tank or loose-fit top that I'll cover with a cardigan once I arrive at work. During the warmer months in subtropical New Orleans, I don't expect to arrive in office-ready form, though I'm fascinated by the number of women I've observed commuting in even the hottest weather who somehow manage to step off their bikes and head straight into the office looking like Audrey Hepburn.

When the heat index soars past 90-degrees, I tend to bring my work clothes in a bag and don athletic clothes—generally, a sports bra, tank top, and a pair of capri running tights, which I sometimes cover with a stretchy skirt—all of which are completely soaked through at the end of my ride. Fortunately, the bike rack at my office is placed near a back door that allows me to step inconspicuously inside and head straight for the changing room.

By carefully folding or rolling my clothes into my pannier, I usually have plenty of space for all that I need to wear to work, and my outfit arrives relatively wrinkle-free. Suit folders are a good option for bike commuting if your workplace requires more formal attire. You could also leave office staples like a blazer and pair of dress shoes at the office to minimize the amount of clothing you need to carry on your bike.

THE BEST FABRICS FOR BIKING

When the temperature and humidity soar, I tend to stick to fast-drying, sweat-wicking, synthetic fabrics. Despite its many virtues, in hot weather, cotton is not always ideal for biking thanks to its absorbent properties. In colder weather, thin wool tops work great for layering. Wool is well-known for its warming properties, but it also boasts breathability, anti-bacterial, and moisture-wicking qualities.

If you live in a place that's especially hot, you might try sticking a slightly dampened shirt or a bandana in the freezer before you go to bed and donning it before you head out on your bike the next morning. This is a trick I've used to stay cooler for other outdoor activities in the summer months too.

WINTER RIDING

Having lived most of my life in the South, I have exactly zero ability to withstand any sort of cold effectively. I bring a sweater with me when I leave the house even in the summer, a function of my cold-intolerance and also the over exuberant use of air conditioning. It's not until I drive others around in my car that I remember that my air conditioner has been broken for years.

Despite my general aversion to cold, I actually prefer biking when it's cold out. I use that term loosely, because in New Orleans, cold means it's below 60-degrees and that I can ride to work without working up a sweat. What we call winter, Minneapolis calls spring. And that's an important comparison, because Minneapolis boasts one of the highest bike-commute rates in the country.

In fall and winter, a warm jacket and gloves worn with my usual bike-commuting garb typically provide all the warmth I need. But on those rare days when the temperature hovers in the 40s or below, I do lots of layering. A typical cold-weather bicycling ensemble for me consists of ankle-length tights, wool socks, thick gloves, a hat that fits under my helmet, a sweat-wicking base layer made of wool or some synthetic fabric, and a fitted athletic jacket.

Layers are essential for me not just to combat the cold but because even on cooler days, I get warm as I ride. I peel off a layer at just about every stoplight, until I'm often down to just a short-sleeved shirt and attracting some quizzical looks from the drivers stopped next to me, bundled in hats and scarves with their heaters on full blast.

I'm less concerned by the cold in winter as I am with the dwindling daylight. When the days are shorter, I get to work and leave

the office a little earlier to avoid biking in low-light situations. I also take care that my lights are working properly (I like to add an extra blinking light to the back of my helmet or shirt) and that I wear light-colored, reflective clothing.

America's Car Dependency
& the Paradigm Shift Underway

"What are streets? For 7,000 years since our cities first were formed, streets had a very singular definition. They were the space in which we transported ourselves, of course, but also the space in which we met, gathered, talked to our neighbors, gossiped. Where we sold our goods. Where our children played. They were extensions of our homes, of our living rooms. They were public domain. Probably the most democratic spaces in the history of Homo sapiens. Now a lot of people seem to have this perception that streets are the exclusive domain of automobiles."

-Mikael Colville-Andersen, CEO of Copenhagenize Design Company[75]

"Freedom to my parents meant having a car. Freedom to my kids means not being dependent on a car."
-R.T. Rybak, former mayor of Minneapolis[76]

"The pattern of the thing precedes the thing."
-Vladimir Nabokov[77]

$\mathcal{M}$y grandmother, Audrey Fontenot Leftwich, known to her grandchildren as Meme, was three years old when she encountered her first car. My great aunt, Anna Fontenot Foret, was in the third grade. It was 1935, and the sisters distinctly remember their father pulling up to the family's farm in rural southwest Louisiana in a big, black Plymouth. With its elongated hood pinched together in the middle and oversized fenders that exaggerated the size of the wheel base, when you blinked it looked a bit like a car that had swallowed a horse and buggy—which had been, up until that time, the Fontenot family's primary mode of conveyance. Otherwise, the Fontenot children and their friends got around the way our ancestors have since the dawn of human civilization: they walked.

As I talk to my grandmother and her sister about some of their earliest memories, my mom chimes in. She recalls a housekeeper named Pearl who would come to her family's house in the late 1950s to help my grandmother with the ironing. She arrived, as was apparently not uncommon at the time among people of Pearl's socioeconomic status in the small town where my mom grew up, by horse and buggy.

I bring up this little bit of family history because it highlights just how very closely tethered we are, chronologically speaking, to the era when cars were not the dominate force that they are today. Although it's easy to think of our car culture as a fact of life that has always been and always will be, in reality, the car has only been commonplace for the tiniest speck in time.

Case in point: many of us have living relatives who can testify to an era when streets were not primarily the domain of fast-moving motor vehicles, but instead were filled with pedestrians, bicyclists, children, vendors, horse-drawn vehicles, and streetcars.

At the turn of the 20th century, automobiles were pricey and rare, a luxury reserved for the rich.[78] But the picture began to shift dramatically beginning in 1908 with the release of Henry Ford's Model T, a vehicle designed for affordability and to appeal to the masses. It was a marketing strategy that proved highly successful. In 1917, there were 5.1 million motor vehicles registered in the U.S.; six years later, that number had expanded threefold.[79]

The car promised unprecedented mobility, convenience, and speed. But it also posed an existential threat to the other occupants of the urban landscape. Auto-related fatalities skyrocketed from around 500 in 1907 to nearly 16,000 in 1923.[80] By 1925, the automobile was responsible for two-thirds of all fatalities in cities larger than 25,000 people.[81] Newspaper headlines and letters to the editor screamed of the mass bloodshed in the streets being wrought by the automobile.

"The horrors of war appear to be less appalling than the horrors of peace," declared a 1924 article in the *New York Times*.[82] The double-page spread was accompanied by an image of the Grim Reaper driving a monstrous, hulking automobile over piles of helpless, rightfully-terrified people. It continued: "The automobile looms as a far more destructive piece of machinery than the machine gun. The reckless motorist deals more death than the artilleryman. The man in the street seems less safe than the man in the trench."

Competition for access to the public rights of way produced dramatic tensions in those early days of the automobile. In his book *Fighting Traffic: The Dawn of the Motor Age in the American City*, historian Peter Norton describes the battle waged in the streets over this point and the massive shift not just in the physical environment but also in the public consciousness required to make way for the automobile.[83]

"Until the 1920s, under prevailing conceptions of the street, cars were at best uninvited guests," Norton writes. "To many they were unruly intruders."[84] But by 1930, a "new street equilibrium" had been reached, he argues, one in which most people "agreed, readily or grudgingly, that streets were chiefly motor thoroughfares, open to others only under carefully defined restrictions."[85]

Whereas Americans initially laid the fault for automobile-related deaths squarely in the laps of the automobile industry, increasingly, the blame came to be placed on the streets' non-motorized users.[86] The concept of jaywalking is a product of this period in American history, Norton notes, a label propagated by the automobile lobby that likened those taking part in a once-routine part of city life—crossing the street at the most convenient location—to country bumpkins.

Over the succeeding decades, American car culture firmly took root. At the 1939 and 1940 World's Fair held in New York, General Motors outlined in its popular Futurama exhibit its vision for a 1960 that was marked by fast-moving, auto-filled highways that would shuttle once-cramped city dwellers away from central business districts to spacious, single-family homes in tranquil suburbs. It was a blueprint that proved to be eerily prescient.[87]

The rise of the car meant that Americans were no longer tethered to streetcar lines, or to the compact, walkable environments that defined human settlement patterns for thousands of years previously. Following World War II, an explosion in housing demand created by returning troops and the beginnings of the baby boom, along with federal policies that promoted new, single-family homes on the periphery of cities where land was abundant and cheap, further entrenched America's reliance on the automobile.

These pressures worked in tandem with school desegregation, white flight, and the construction of the interstate highway system, authorized by President Dwight Eisenhower in 1956, to lure huge numbers of Americans to modern lifestyles built entirely around the automobile.

The more prevalent the car became, the more geographically disconnected became the places we lived from our day-to-day needs, the more dependent we became on our automobiles, and the more dangerous the streets became for anyone not riding in one. School transportation statistics help to illustrate this dramatic shift. In 1969, nearly half of all kindergarten through eighth-grade-aged children walked or biked to school; by 2009, just thirteen percent of American children in that age range did so.[88] Even among those living within a mile of school, just more than one-third walked or biked to school in 2009, compared with 85 percent in 1969.[89]

As Jeff Speck, an urban designer and the author of *Walkable City* puts it, the automobile that was once perceived as a mechanism of freedom has become a "gas-belching, time-wasting, and life-threatening prosthetic device that many of us—most Americans in fact—need just to live our lives."[90] Nowhere is this more evident than in America's suburbs. While many of this country's older cities retain key features of their pre-automobile origins—pedestrian scale, neighborhood stores, relatively functional transit systems—most of the nation's newer communities grew up around the automobile.

American central cities and their suburbs experienced rapid growth between 1910 and 1930, but by 1940, suburbs were where most of the growth was occurring. As of 1960, the proportion of U.S. residents living in suburbs was roughly equal to the proportion of central city dwellers, but by the year 2000, half of all Americans lived in suburbs while just 30 percent lived in the urban core.[91]

Cities hemorrhaging their populations struggled to keep pace with their suburban counterparts. Streets were widened to make way for the automobile. Streetcar lines were ripped out and decommissioned. Downtown buildings were torn down to accommodate acres of asphalt parking lots. Interstate freeways decimated the historic and culture fabric of urban centers across the country, stoking massive protests and debate that pitted preservationists and social equity advocates against those touting the new tools of progress and modernity.

"Almost every city is split down the middle today between the need for new traffic arteries and the displacement and blight that the giant roadways seem to bring in their wake," noted a 1967 newspaper article on the subject.[92] "The [interstate highway] program has sent giant rivers of concrete creeping like lava through residential neighborhoods and commercial areas, dislocating families, schools, churches and businesses," described another.[93]

In New Orleans, a proposal first developed in the 1940s by powerful New York highwayman Robert Moses and known as the Riverfront Expressway was typical of the period. The six-lane, 40-foot elevated highway was to edge the French Quarter, flanking the famed Jackson Square, originally laid out in 1721, with a massive new 20th century symbol of automobile supremacy. The project was embraced by the economic and political elite and polarized the city.

"The Riverfront Expressway ... will supplement and nourish the giant skyscrapers we are constructing," New Orleans Mayor Victor Schiro declared. "The old ways in New Orleans are finished and done away with. New Orleans is on the march."[94]

Ultimately, the Riverfront Expressway project was scuttled in 1969 thanks to the work of an ardent band of historic preservationists and a last-minute reprieve from U.S. Transportation Secretary John Volpe, who, in denying federal funds for the freeway, explained that he did not believe that the anticipated benefits from the highway would justify decimating the French Quarter.[95] It was one of the first times federal funds had been denied a highway program on historic preservation grounds, and it was heralded as a shift in course in American transportation planning that had for decades privileged traffic flow above almost any other consideration. The *New York Times* editorial board proclaimed the move "an indication from the Secretary of Transportation that we need not, after all, accept the concrete cloverleaf as the national flower."[96]

Even as the nation's highway-building frenzy began to wane in the late 1960s and 1970s, it has given rise to a car dependence that will be difficult to shake.

In the year 2000, the U.S. boasted the highest rate of automobile ownership of any other country, and the vast majority of trips, even among the poor, were made by personal automobile.[97]

Today, however, there are important signs of shifts underway in public policy and consumer preferences that fundamentally influence where we live and how we get around.

The United States has for more than a decade seen significant federal investment in policies and programs that support bicycling and walking. According to an analysis by John Pucher, Ralph Buehler, and Mark Seinen, federal funding for active transportation has increased substantially with each new federal transportation bill passed in the 1990s and 2000s.[98]

Whereas the US allocated an average of just $5 million annually toward bicycling and walking from 1988 to 1990, that figure rose to an average $150 million per year from 1992 to 1998, then again to an average of $360 million per year from 1999 to 2005, and to close to $1 billion under legislation adopted in 2005.[99] The Moving Ahead for Progress in the 21st Century Act, or MAP-21, the transportation bill signed into law by President Obama in 2012 and under which the federal government continues to operate as I write this, was roundly criticized by bicycle and pedestrian advocates for its restructuring of the program that funded active transportation programs, giving states more flexibility as to how they spent money previously set aside for these activities exclusively. As of 2013, a total of $809 million was allocated to the Transportation Alternatives Program, whereas in 2011, under the previous transportation bill, $1.2 billion was allocated to three separate programs now consolidated under the TAP.[100] [101]

Despite the dip, bicycling and walking funding remains well above where it stood in the recent past. The percentage of overall federal transportation funding allocated to biking and walking programs increased from 1.6 percent in 2010 to 2.1 percent in 2014.[102] That investment has had substantial effect in encouraging local governments to build bike facilities and programs. There are no national statistics on the number of bicycle facilities in the US, but figures from the Rails to Trails Conservancy showing substantial expansion in projects that turn abandoned railroad rights of way into biking and walking trails across the country serve as a useful proxy.[103] The total number of rail trails in the country has risen from 2,044 miles in 1990 to 22,050 as of 2015.[104] [105] Moreover, the Alliance for Biking & Walking reports that as of 2014, more than half of all states and cities in the US have "complete streets" policies or laws in place, requiring policy makers to at least consider users other than drivers in constructing new transportation projects. [106]

These new facilities, programs, and policies are undoubtedly having an impact. "Well-designed bicycle infrastructure will seduce people to use it," says Mikael Colville-Andersen, CEO of Copenhagenize Design Company, which specializes in bicycle-related planning and design.[107] "You make the bicycle the quickest way from A to B in a city ... and citizens will ride, seduced by the good design, the convenience, and the safety."

Yes, the car remains the king of America's transportation system, but the past several years have brought a substantial increase in the proportion of people getting around by active means.

As of the most recent national survey conducted in 2009, the bike is used for about one percent of all trips nationwide.[108] Although this figure is a far cry from the rates seen in a number of other industrialized nations and just a slight increase from the previous national survey in 2001, a growing body of evidence suggests that the bike is viewed as an increasingly viable mode of transportation, especially in large urban areas.[109]

Commute to work statistics tracked annually by the U.S. Census Bureau provide a glimpse into the shift. While a mere 0.62 percent of the American working public got to work by bike as of the 2013 American Community Survey estimate, the number of people who get to work by bike increased between 2000 and 2013 by 62 percent to 882,198, a larger increase than experienced by any other mode.[110]

The rather paltry national bike commute statistic masks a far more substantial rate of bicycling for transportation taking shape in a number of cities across the country, many of which have invested substantially in new infrastructure. Cities like Washington, D.C., Pittsburg, Memphis, Portland, and New Orleans have witnessed bike-commuting growth that far outpaces the national rate of growth by double, triple, or more. Forty-one of the country's 70 largest cities have bike commute rates that exceed the national average, in some cases by substantial margins.[111]

Portland stood as the large city with the highest share of bike commuters as of the 2013 ACS, with 5.9 percent of its workforce getting to the job by bike. But among the nation's 70 largest cities, Washington, D.C., San Francisco, Tucson, Oakland, Minneapolis, New Orleans, and Seattle also had bike commute rates of at least three percent, a rate that no large American city achieved as of the year 2000.[112][113] Meantime, a majority of Americans say they would like to bike more, but most also say they are held back by their fears of the dangers of biking: namely, being hit by a car.[114]

Americans are more apt to walk than bike for transportation, and although walk commuting has declined in recent decades, it too has recently experienced a resurgence. The rate of Americans walking to work stood at 5.6 in 1980 and had dipped to 2.9 percent in 2000, but starting in 2005, the national walk commute rate started to rebound.[115] [116] It now hovers at about three percent.[117]

Meantime, we are driving less, a reversal of an upward trajectory building for the past 60 years.[118] The decline in driving preceded the Great Recession, causing some observers to posit that the change related not to lingering economic concerns but to something more structural.[119]

"Has the developed world reached 'peak car'?" asked the headline on a recent analysis by the asset management firm Schroders.[120] Michael Sivak, a researcher at the University of Michigan's Transportation Research Institute, says it's quite possible. He notes that the rates of automobile ownership, distance driven, and licensed drivers reached their peak around 2004.[121] "One cannot ascribe the decrease that we are observing to economic factors only," he said.[122]

Many young people are postponing driver's licenses or opting not to get them at all.[123] Whereas 87 percent of nineteen-year-olds had driver's licenses in the mid-1990s, fewer than 70 percent of nineteen-year-olds had them in 2014.[124] Schroders' Katherine Davidson credits this change to the growing appeal of urban living and the rise of smartphones and e-commerce, all of which reduce the need to drive.[125]

Sivak's group conducted a survey of 600 people without driver's licenses between the ages of 18 and 39 aimed at finding out more about those postponing automobility. Respondents asked why they didn't have a license gave a range of answers. Some didn't consider driving that important, or preferred walking or biking to get places, while others expressed concern about the costs of owning and operating an automobile. Most fascinating to Sivak was the 22 percent of respondents who said they never planned to get a driver's license.[126] "This is obviously of concern to the auto industry," he said.[127]

A 2014 Nielsen study found that a majority of millennials, the generation of people born from the early 1980s to the mid 1990s that is quickly overtaking baby boomers as the most populace living generation, expressed a preference for communities that lend themselves to navigation by means other than driving.[128] It further found that in 2011, 66 percent of millennials under 25 owned a car, compared with 73 percent in 2007.[129] Statistics such as these prompted Davidson to conclude that for many young people "cars are not as relevant as a status symbol, and getting a license is no longer a 'rite of passage' the way it once was."[130]

A growing desire for walkable, bikeable, transit-friendly places is most likely helping to spur what many have heralded as the resurgence of the city. Once relegated to the poor and disenfranchised, urban living environments that offer a strong sense of place and a variety of amenities accessible via means other than the automobile are once again places where lots of people want to be.

"Cities are back," declared Ellen Dunham-Jones, an architect and urban designer and the author of *Retrofitting Suburbia*, at a recent lecture I attended. She pointed to dying suburban shopping malls, mounting suburban office vacancy rates, and a return to the city of corporations that decades ago fled the city in favor of the suburbs, among other indicators of the changes underway.[131]

Even as a slight majority (51 percent) of Americans were living in the suburbs as of the 2010 Census, one-third of the country's population was concentrated in cities, the largest proportion since 1950.[132] Based on the first three years of estimates released since the 2010 Census, growth in cities exceeded city growth rates seen from 2000-2010.[133]

Unlike the previous decade and several decades prior, central city growth was outpacing that of suburbs in metro areas with more than one million people.[134] "It raises the question, 'Is this city growth revival here to stay?'" wrote Brookings Institution demographer William Frey. "Or is it a lingering symptom of the recession, mortgage meltdown and the plight of still stuck in place young adults?"[135]

Another analysis found that jobs that have for some time been concentrating in outlying areas appear to be following people back to the city. Looking at 2007-2011 Census data, Joe Cortright of the Portland-based think tank City Observatory found that areas within three miles of a metro region's central business district were outpacing surrounding areas in terms of job growth in more than half of 41 of the largest U.S. metro areas evaluated.[136] "This 'center-led' growth represents the reversal of a historic trend of job de-centralization that has persisted for the past half century," Cortright wrote. "As recently as 2002-2007, peripheral areas were growing much faster … and aggregate job growth was stagnant in urban areas." Over the past several years, corporations including Zappos, Coca Cola, Amazon, and VISA have expanded in or relocated to city centers.[137]

The changes are evident in my own city, which has long suffered the effects of outmigration and suburban flight, but is seeing a resurgence, with new high rise apartments being constructed in previously burned-out buildings downtown, and prices skyrocketing in dense urban neighborhoods that within my recent memory were peeling, crime- and poverty-stricken places whose primary appeal was affordability and central location. A recent city auction of New Orleans residential properties with outstanding tax bills attracted a flurry of interest and bids, especially in the urban core.[138] "Though the neighborhoods remain largely poor, they are rapidly gentrifying as many well-to-do residents, especially millennials, eschew the suburbs in search of 'authentic' New Orleans," wrote reporter Robert McClendon of the phenomenon.[139]

The shift back to cities very well could be a short-lived pattern that will soon correct itself in favor of suburban supremacy. As I write this, new Census estimates suggest that exurban areas, those far-flung places beyond even the more traditional, closer-in suburbs, are once again growing faster than the urban core. The data caused Frey to wonder whether the last few years of urban growth may have been an anomaly, even as he doesn't expect a rebound of the type of unchecked suburban growth we have witnessed in decades past.[140] Yet while it is certainly too early to write off the suburbs, key demographic shifts are changing the face of our metropolitan regions and carry important implications for the future shape of our cities.

For one thing, as Dunham-Jones argues, America's suburbs were built for families that don't exist anymore. Since 2000, she notes, two-thirds of suburban households have been childless.[141] Aging empty nesters are left with an abundance of space in cul-de-sac communities in which it is difficult to access everyday needs without driving, leaving them isolated and dependent on cars they won't be able to drive indefinitely. Meantime, on the other end of the age spectrum, many millennials grew up in the suburbs, but desire the trappings of urban life.[142] Simultaneously, Americans are putting off marriage and children longer than did previous generations, and may not see the urgency in heading out to the suburbs to raise families in the land of better schools and big back yards.[143]

Moreover, the unintended tolls of suburban life are increasingly apparent in terms of public health, the environment, and personal checking accounts. The suburbs were built as the halcyon antidote to the crowded, disease- and crime-ridden city, but today's major health threats include the rising epidemic of chronic disease related to obesity and inactivity. "There is," Dunham-Jones says, "a correlation between suburban sprawl and human sprawl."[144] Meantime, automobile crashes rate[I] as the number one killer of Americans between the ages of five and thirty-five.[145]

"In the U.S., we design so that people can go as fast as they desire," said Norm Garrick, associate professor of civil and environmental engineering at the University of Connecticut.[146] " ...The change in Sweden and other places in Europe such as The Netherlands is that we need to design for safety, we need to design for context." Mounting concern about safety on America's roadways, combined with growing recognition of the economic, equity, environmental, and quality of life challenges posed by our automobile reliance are creating a mounting impetus to do things differently.

In 2014, U.S. Transportation Secretary Anthony Foxx announced a new push by his agency to improve the transportation landscape, especially for the most vulnerable users.[147] "Safety is our highest priority and that commitment is the same regardless of which form of transportation people choose," Foxx said.[148] In 2015, Foxx unveiled his "Mayor's Challenge for Safer People and Safer Streets," a challenge to cities across the country to improve the landscape for pedestrians and bicyclists.[149]

A growing number of mostly large American cities—New York, Boston, Los Angeles, Chicago, Washington, D.C., Portland, San Francisco, and Seattle among them—have taken a cue from Sweden and adopted or announced plans to adopt Vision Zero policies, lofty goals of reducing transportation-related fatalities.[150][151] As part of this effort, some are lowering speed limits with the goal of reducing the frequency and severity of crashes, challenging the long-accepted notion that the streets are for funneling cars as quickly and efficiently as possible.[152][153]

"Most city planners now see the era of the car's urban supremacy as a brief, misguided phase in city culture," writer Susan Dominus declared in a piece on growing concern about pedestrian safety in New York City.[154] And while I'm not sure that this is yet the case outside this country's largest cities, I think it's true that nationwide there is a detectable, if sometimes subtle, shift taking place in the public discourse where our streets are concerned.

Ethical imperatives, environmental concerns, and shifting personal preferences aside, I think another factor bodes well for growing investment in alternatives to driving: we're running out of money and space for roads. The gas tax, contrary to popular opinion, doesn't actually cover the costs of building our roads and bridges, much of the burden for which is covered by general funds to which we all contribute through sales and property taxes, whether we drive or not.[155] Transportation costs are increasingly burdensome on users, especially for those living in far-flung places completely reliant on the automobile, and particularly for the poor who are increasingly those populating the suburbs.[156] Meantime, traffic congestion is worsening, and things are only expected to get worse. "Over the next 30 years, we're going to have 70 million more people in this country, and all of those people are going to be trying to get someplace, on top of the number we have," Secretary Foxx told NPR.[157] "So the congestion we have today is expected to get worse unless we do something radically different now."

This much is certain: widening or building more roads isn't the solution to our congestion woes, costs notwithstanding. More roads mean more cars and more driving. It is a phenomenon known as induced demand, one that started to be recognized as it applies to road building in the 1960s and that is increasingly panning out.[158] In 2009, economists Matthew Turner of the University of Toronto and Gilles Duranton of the University of Pennsylvania investigated the relationship between new roads and highways built in cities across the U.S. between 1983 and 2003 and the number of miles driven in those cities. They found a one-to-one relationship between roads and driving.[159] Correlation doesn't necessarily imply causation, but the researchers argue that their analysis confirms "the fundamental law of traffic congestion," a paradox first identified decades earlier by economist Anthony Downs. It holds, in short, that "the extension of most major roads is met with a proportional increase in traffic."[160]

Given just how steeped we have become in our car-centric ways, it shouldn't be surprising that the recent resurgence in bicycling in particular has given rise to a strong resistance in certain quarters. Few topics can rile up the comments section in my local newspaper or a dinner party conversation like bicycling. I am reminded of an email I received from a relative a while back containing a link to a diatribe about the looming "bike wars." Be forewarned, was the author's message: the bicyclists are coming after your neighborhood—and your parking spaces. It was the simplistic, fear mongering drivel one might expect from a chain letter written in different fonts and colors and instructing the reader to forward it to *at least twenty people* or risk imminent death. Instead, it came from the esteemed pages of the *Wall Street Journal*.[161]

Incidentally, it is not some monolithic special interest group pushing for improved accommodations for people who wish to get around by means other than the automobile. Rather, it is a motley group of people ranging in age, race, gender, political persuasion, and geographic representation. It includes parents, public health advocates, environmentalists, educators, economists, economic development professionals, advocates for the poor and disabled, real estate developers, and even the AARP.

There is a part of me that gets where the discomfort comes from. Although America has not always been a car culture, our car-centric roots run deep. Ours is a country in which those who can afford to drive have hopped into their cars and gotten relatively quickly (and cheaply, compared to many developed countries) wherever they wanted to go. The attitude born of our recent history is that automobiles are and forever will be the unquestioned rulers of our streets. Until I started bicycling, I too held tighter to this belief than I recognized. I take solace in remembering that the tensions are the result of real change afoot, and

Hand Signals

There are a couple of versions of hand signals used by bicyclists. I prefer the following signals, which I think are the simplest to remember and the easiest for other road users to understand:

or

TURNING RIGHT:
Extend your right arm and point in that direction.

TURNING LEFT:
Extend your left arm and point in that direction.

STOPPING: Bend your left arm at a right angle to your body with your hand pointing toward the ground, palm facing behind you.

that the more people who take to walking, biking, and riding transit in their communities, even if occasionally, the more acceptance for this new, old paradigm there will be.

Bicycling in Traffic

Unless you live in one of those rare places criss-crossed by miles and miles of protected bikeways, chances are, getting around on your bike will necessitate riding in traffic. The good news is that if you're a driver, you already know most of the rules of the road for bicycling. Bicycles in the U.S. are considered vehicles, are subject to many of the same responsibilities and rights of motor-vehicles, and are allowed on any roadway not marked as off-limits to bicyclists (U.S. interstates are among the routes where bicyclists are usually prohibited).

With few exceptions, bicyclists are expected to ride in the direction of traffic, to obey traffic signals, and to yield to pedestrians. In many jurisdictions, it's illegal for adults to bike on the sidewalk, so check your local laws.

There are several bike-specific rules of the road that can help you to more safely navigate the streets:

RIDE AS FAR TO THE RIGHT AS PRACTICABLE

On roads that lack bike lanes, bicyclists in the U.S. are generally expected to ride as far to the right of the rightmost travel lane as "practicable." The meaning of this directive is the subject of confusion and debate, but I found a satisfying definition in Bob Mionske's book *Bicycling & the Law*. Mionske, a lawyer, interprets this to mean "as close to the right as can reasonably be accomplished under the circumstances." The League of American Bicyclists boils it down even more simply, advising that bicyclists generally occupy the right one-third of the lane, taking care to avoid the curb and other potential hazards.

In most states, it is also acceptable under certain circumstances for a bicyclist to "take the lane," or ride in the center of the travel lane.

(continued on page 106)

The Importance of (Mostly) Following Traffic Rules on Your Bike

You will often be tempted to break the rules on your bike.

It may seem, as it did for me when I first started riding regularly, that taking such liberties as sailing through stop signs, rolling through red lights, and riding the wrong way down city streets are among the perks of leaving your car at home. And depending on where you live, you may notice that many bicyclists do all of these things with frequency—and to seemingly little consequence.

Sometimes, there are very good reasons why people on bikes may choose to disobey traffic laws. Most traffic rules were created for motor vehicles and some of them are particularly ill-suited to bicyclists' realities. In many cases, bad design neglects—or addresses only as an afterthought—bicyclists' needs.

Even today, to avoid an especially hostile arterial, I will on occasion (paying very close attention to oncoming traffic and to what's going on at intersections) ride a couple blocks in the wrong direction on a one-way street or take the sidewalk, even though both of these maneuvers are illegal where I live. Other times, when no one is stopped at the other intersections adjacent to me, I will scoot through a stop sign. (In some places, this maneuver, often referred to as the Idaho Rule, is perfectly legal, and takes into account the challenges of coming to a complete stop on a bike, starting up again and regaining a good speed quickly.)

But generally speaking, obeying traffic rules on your bike is not only in the interest of your personal safety. I would argue that it's also in the best interest of the broader bicycling community. Your personal health aside, like it or not, every time you ride your bike on the street, you are acting as a spokeswoman for bicyclists everywhere.

Taking the lane is a viable option when:

1. A bicyclist is riding in a lane that is too narrow to share with an automobile
2. A bicyclist is riding at the same speed as motorized traffic
3. A bicyclist is preparing to turn left
4. A row of parked cars is taking up the bike lane

Taking the lane can be intimidating at first, but it is ultimately quite empowering. It can also be safer than hewing too closely to the edge of a lane, which can encourage drivers to squeeze dangerously close by to pass.

Other reasons you might stray from the right-most portion of the lane include avoiding a hazard, such as a pothole, an opening car door, debris in the roadway, or avoiding a designated turn lane. If you're traveling straight through an intersection marked with a right-turn lane, you should stay to the left of the turn lane in the right-most through-travel lane.

RIDE IN A STRAIGHT LINE

Ride in a manner that makes it clear to drivers what your intentions are and what your next move is likely to be. Other road users will be better able to predict your next move if you ride in a straight line.

On roads without bike lanes, it may seem like a good idea to weave in and out of cars parked in a parking lane to avoid vehicles coming up from behind. In reality, riding in a smooth, consistent manner and not hugging the edge of the road too closely is the better way to go, making it easier for drivers to see you and anticipate your behavior. Try to ride in the lane, a few feet away from its edge, and take some solace in knowing that in urban areas, crashes resulting from automobiles running into cyclists from behind are relatively rare. A simple rear-view mirror that allows you to see what drivers behind you are up to can make this practice far less daunting.

USE HAND SIGNALS

Use hand signals (shown in sidebar on page 102) and check before changing lanes or making a turn to make sure it's safe to do so.

BE ALERT AT INTERSECTIONS

Bicyclists need to develop a sixth sense for avoiding hazards, especially those lurking around intersections. Intersections are the places where most crashes involving bicyclists occur in urban areas. The right hook is one of the most common types of crashes; situations in which drivers making a right turn pull into or in front of bicyclists, often suddenly and unexpectedly.

{ maneuvering around a turning lane }

Always be alert for drivers and road users who may fail to stop, who are turning and may not be looking for you, who are pulling out of driveways, or who may not see you because of some obstruction, like another car. Remember that even if you legally have the right of way, you're likely to be the one to suffer the biggest consequences in a crash.

I like to slow down at intersections even when I have the right of way to make sure that drivers are going to stop for me. It's a good idea to look drivers in the eye where possible. If you see a driver inching out into an intersection with their head turned away from you or their eyes cast downward into the glow of a cell phone, chances are good that they have no idea you're there. I also like to wait a few seconds after a light turns green before moving into an intersection to account for red-light runners. When riding through an intersection along a multi-lane roadway, be sure that all lanes of traffic are stopped for you before you cross. A dangerous situation can present itself when the car closest to you stops, only to shield you from view of another approaching vehicle.

AVOID THE DOOR ZONE

When riding on a street alongside a row of parked cars, keep far enough left to avoid the "door zone," the space that an open door would occupy. Legally, drivers are expected to pay attention to avoid opening car doors onto an approaching cyclist, but given the number of cyclists I know who have been injured in just this way, it doesn't seem that many of them actually do. Even if you're riding in a bike lane, be alert for car doors that may open into your path and try to leave at least four feet of space between your body and a row of parked cars. You should also watch for illuminated brake lights on cars parked in the lane parallel to you as you ride, which are a telltale sign that an opening door is imminent or that a driver is preparing to move out of a parking space.

PASS ON THE LEFT

When passing another cyclist, pass on the left. It's also customary and polite to vocalize your intentions with a friendly "passing on your left." You can also ding your bell as you approach to keep the other cyclist apprised of your movements.

PUT YOUR VOCAL CHORDS TO WORK

Don't be shy about using your voice. It's one of your greatest tools when riding a bike. A loudly-pronounced "on your left" or "on your right" is sometimes all it takes to get the attention of a distracted driver who may not notice that you are riding in a space that they are attempting to enter. I find these verbal cues especially useful at spots where bike lanes and bike paths intersect with roadways, where drivers often look only toward oncoming automobile traffic or to the light in front of them, neglecting to check for approaching bicyclists and pedestrians.

CROSS RAIL TRACKS AT A 90-DEGREE ANGLE

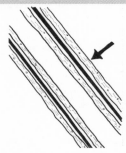

Rail lines may or may not be something you encounter with frequency in your city, but in places with lots of streetcar tracks or other rail infrastructure, it's important to ride across grade-level tracks carefully, with your tires at a right angle to the tracks, to avoid getting them stuck and causing you to topple over.

EXPECT THE UNEXPECTED

No matter where you're riding, remember that even when you're following the rules, you need to pay very close attention to what's going on around you. Even dedicated bike facilities aren't guaranteed protection, to say nothing of your typical city street.

Be a Safe Driver

An unexpected side effect of my bike habit is that I've become a far more conscientious driver. I won't text and drive, I always stop at crosswalks, and I'm generally far more aware of the fact that I'm driving around in a potentially-lethal, two-ton weapon.

Familiarize yourself with the laws governing driver behavior around cyclists and pedestrians. Although drivers don't have a great reputation among many bicyclists (and vice versa), the culture is changing rapidly in many places, thanks in part to the growing numbers of cyclists on the streets and the fact that increasingly, drivers are cyclists too or have friends and relatives who are.

If You're Involved in a Crash

Call 911. When the police arrive, be sure that they write an accident report. Document the scene and any damages or injuries by taking photographs if possible. Get the names and contact information of the driver and any witnesses on the scene. Exchange insurance information with the driver.

Try to write down or memorize the vehicle license plate right away, in case the driver leaves the scene. Get a good physical description of the vehicle if possible. If necessary, contact a lawyer. An expanding number of American lawyers now specialize in protecting bicyclists' rights.

Some automobile policies will cover injuries or damages suffered by a customer while riding a bike. In the unfortunate case of a hit-and-run, your uninsured motorist coverage in some cases may be applied.

Making a Left Turn

To make a left turn, you can maneuver similarly to the way you would in a car: signal, then carefully merge into the left-most lane and make your turn. But a technique that can be somewhat less harrowing, especially in situations where fast-moving traffic or moving across multiple lanes make left turns difficult, is alternatively referred to as the "Copenhagen Left" or box turn. Instead of turning immediately left, you'll move straight through the intersection (on alert for any right-turning cars that may not be watching for you), stop at the other side, turn your bike 90-degrees to the left, then proceed straight through. This sounds complicated but it can make left turns much easier and less scary.

DRIVER'S ED

Pass Only When It's Safe to Do So

Sometimes, you will have to be patient when driving around a bicyclist. The fact is that she is likely to be moving slower than you. Take a deep breath, realize that she is well within her rights in occupying the public right-of-way, and that you are not likely to have to wait for very long for an appropriate opportunity to pass. Imagine yourself in the bicyclist's position, largely unprotected on the road with a two-ton vehicle at your back and anxious to get by. When you do pass, maintain at least three feet between your car and the bicyclist. That's the minimum required by law in most states. Familiarize yourself with the laws in your community.

Don't Honk or Yell at Cyclists

In many places, it is illegal to harass bicyclists. It's also a really bad idea to do so no matter where you find yourself. If a cyclist is riding in front of you in the roadway, she is technically and legally in control of the lane and has as much right to be there as any other vehicle.

Steer Clear of Bike Lanes

Drivers are expected to stay out of bike lanes, with a few exceptions, such as when entering or leaving a street parking space adjacent to a bike lane or preparing to turn at an intersection. Drivers are always required to yield to cyclists when moving into or out of a bike lane.

Check for Cyclists Before Opening Car Doors

When parallel parking on the street, be sure to look before opening your car door to make sure that a bicyclist isn't approaching. One way to avoid dooring a cyclist is by getting into the habit of reaching across your body with your right hand to open your driver's side door. This requires you to turn in such a way that you might be reminded to look out for any approaching bicyclists.

Put Down Your Phone!

BONUS TIPS!

Driving Safely Around Pedestrians

In my city, even as drivers have gotten far more bike-aware, pedestrians often continue to get short shrift. This book is about bicycling, but it's more broadly about the joys of active transportation and experiencing your city at slower cadence than allowed by the automobile. For that reason, I would feel remiss in not pointing out a few tips for driving safely around pedestrians, too:

STOP FOR PEDESTRIANS AT CROSSWALKS

It's the law in most places. Even if an intersection isn't striped with a crosswalk, you should give right-of-way to pedestrians there.

STOP BEFORE THE CROSSWALK

When coming to a stop at an intersection, leave space for pedestrians to cross in front of you. Observation suggests that many drivers are unaware that the thick white "stop bar" present at most signalized intersections is actually intended to guide them to the appropriate stopping point.

WATCH FOR PEDESTRIANS BEFORE TURNING

Often, drivers pay attention only to vehicular traffic when making a turn. Scan your surroundings for pedestrians, too, looking left, right, and ahead to the space into which you're turning. If you've waited several seconds for a gap in traffic, scan your surroundings again before turning.

America's Car Dependency

SIGN LANGUAGE
A Rundown of the Types of Bike Facilities
& How to Use Them

BIKE LANE

These come in a variety of forms, from a simple, continuous striping on a road to lanes separated from the rest of the traffic by a physical barricade (and in this latter form are sometimes called cycletracks). They are intended for use by bicycles exclusively.

MULTI-USE PATH/BIKE TRAIL

These are paths completely separated from motor vehicle traffic, and usually intended for non-motorized users. They are often the domain of recreational bicyclists, walkers, runners and skaters, though they can also serve as important links in a city's active transportation network. When biking these paths, yield right-of-way to pedestrians and slower bicyclists, and anticipate coming into contact with less-experienced users who may not always use the facility predictably or according to the rules.

SHARROW/CHEVRON MARKINGS

Although bicyclists are legally allowed on all roads not expressly designated as off-limits, these markings are sometimes found in places that lack dedicated bike lanes as a reminder to drivers to anticipate bicyclists. They are often used along sections of roads that connect with dedicated bike lanes but that are themselves deemed too narrow for a separated facility.

BIKE BOX

These are dedicated spaces at intersections that allow bicyclists to place themselves ahead of motor-vehicle traffic when stopping. They are designed to make bicyclists' presence more conspicuous to drivers and thereby reduce the likelihood of right-hook crashes.

MAP IT OUT

Once you've decided to start biking for transportation, learned the rules of the road, and gotten your bike and equipment ready, you'll need to figure out how you want to get from point A to point B. You'll quickly discover when riding a bike that you won't always be comfortably following the same route that you would in a car. Some roads are simply far more conducive to bicycling than others.

There are a handful of major connectors I ride almost every time I get on my bike. Not only do these roads get me where I need to go; many are also equipped with bike-friendly infrastructure, or are especially smooth, wide and well-lit, or feature slow-moving traffic, or take me past a favorite coffee shop. I will gladly ride a little bit out of my way if it means a more pleasant, safe trip.

Ask friends, colleagues, bike shop employees, and members of your local bicycle advocacy organization which routes they find best for bicycling and how they get to key points around town. Look at maps of your city's road and bikeway network and try Googling your route.

Google Maps now features suggested bike routes for an expanding number of cities and towns, but they are just suggestions and are not always ideal.

You might also check to see if your city has any "bike trains" in operation. These are organized group bike rides that help people get where they need to go.

Prior to setting out on bike for the first time, I'd suggest driving your potential route or riding it with a friend to make sure you don't encounter any unforeseen obstacles that would make biking there unappealing. You might also figure out if any useful transit connections exist in the vicinity of your potential route that might be useful if your bike breaks down unexpectedly.

Watch out for left turning vehicles and vehicles in multiple lanes!

Changing Gears

Even as they're not always necessary, depending on the topography of your city, gears can come in quite handy even in super-flat locales. They can aid in powering up hills or overpasses, riding against the wind on an especially blustery day, and in starting up again after stopping.

In lower gears, you'll be able to pedal more easily, but you'll also have to pedal much faster than you would in a higher gear to generate speed. In higher gears, the opposite is true: it's harder to pedal, but you'll go faster at a lower pedal cadence.

Start out in a lower gear and move into a higher gear after you get going to increase your speed, just as you would in a manual-transmission car. It's also a good idea to shift into lower gears when stopping at a light or stop sign so that when you start again, it's less of a struggle and easier on your bike and your knees.

OPERATING YOUR GEARS

To operate the simple gear system on my three-gear city bike, I only have to twist the shifter on my handlebars. For most of my ride to work, I use the third gear, which is the largest, unless I'm climbing an overpass or coming to a stop, in which case I'll shift into a lower gear.

Many performance road bikes are equipped with ten gears or more that are controlled by dual shifters located on both sides of the bike, either on the tops or tips of the handlebars or on the down tube. The left shifter moves the chain on the front-most ring near the pedals. The right lever, as process of elimination suggests, changes the position of the chain on the rear wheel. Because I don't ride a road bike all that often, I keep my gear shifters straight with the memory aid, "Right goes with rear."

If your bike has lever shifters, you'll pull the lever toward your body to shift to a lower (or easier) gear. When you need more tension, you'll push the lever away from your body, toward the handlebars. These dual-shifter gear systems take some experimentation to master. Remember that the overall gear in play depends on the combination of right and left settings. As a rule of thumb, you'll adjust your left shifter to make big changes in your gear setting then use your right shifter to get it just right. When riding a road bike, once I've adjusted my gears the first time, I don't tend to fool with the left shifter much at all.

Tip: Pedal forward while shifting your gears so as not to stress your chain or get it caught in an awkward position.

Don't Forget Your U-lock: Right (and Wrong) Ways to Lock Your Bike

Tools you'll need:
- a sturdy lock
- a fixed, immovable object to lock to

One of the perks of the old beater bike that I used when I first started riding for transportation was that it was a rather unlikely target for bike thieves. In all the years I rode that bike, the lightweight cable lock I kept coiled around its handlebars worked just fine to protect it when it wasn't in use, as proven by the fact that I would return time and again to find my bike right where I left it. In retrospect, I think it was less my lock than luck—and the low resale value of the rusting mountain bike I'd dragged from city to city over a couple of decades—that kept thieves at bay.

CHOOSING A LOCK

Though their portability and the ease with which they can be tethered to objects of a variety of sizes make them appealing, cable locks are notoriously flimsy. You only have to look to YouTube for evidence of the ease with these flexible cable locks are clipped or pried apart. U-locks and chain locks, while not inviolable, offer much better protection, and come with a range of price tags and promises. You can read reviews aplenty about the various choices online. Some manufacturers even offer anti-theft warranties with their pricier selections.

Typically, the clunkier the lock, the more protection it offers, but also the more difficult it is to lug around. Some people attach mounting brackets to their bike frames to transport their U-locks. I generally carry mine around in a pannier. Assuming there's enough room on your seat post, chain locks can be wrapped around the base of your saddle when not in use.

The late (and ever practical) bicycle guru Sheldon Brown proposed an alternative to riding around with a bulky lock in tow. He suggested that regular bike commuters with secure bike parking at home lighten their load by leaving their U-lock at work, tethered to whatever they normally lock their bike to, and toting with them a lightweight cable lock for emergencies or quick errands. (You can read more of Brown's musings on bicycling at his website, sheldonbrown.com, which is posthumously maintained.)

Ideally, you'll want to lock both your frame and a wheel to a bike rack or other fixed object. The back wheel is one of the most valuable components of the typical bike, so you'll generally want to be sure it's the one that gets locked. Some cyclists go so far as to remove the front wheel and lock it together with the back wheel and frame. This might be especially appealing if your wheels are equipped with quick-release mechanisms, and if you'll be parked in an especially high-theft area for a significant amount of time.

I tend to take the easier route, locking the frame and back wheel to the rack with my U-lock. Brown promoted an even simpler technique—one that works equally as well when using a smaller (and consequently lighter) U-lock. According to The Sheldon Method, you need only secure your lock around the rack and the rear wheel somewhere inside the triangle formed by the bike's frame at the rear of your bike. Although you're not technically locking around the frame of the bike, Brown argued that this effectively locks both the wheel and the frame. Using this technique, it would still be possible for a thief to make off with your front wheel, so if you happen to have a double loop cable lock available (one that, unlike those code-based twist locks comes with small loops at either end) and want to make the extra effort, you can help to prevent this fate by securing the cable through the U-lock at one end and wrapping it through your front wheel with the other.

If your destination lacks bicycle racks, look for a sturdy, immovable object to lock your bike to. Good options include lampposts, street signs, steel fences or tall parking meters. Make sure that that your bike and lock cannot be easily slipped over and removed from a post and that you're not locking to something that can be easily clipped, such as the links on a chain-link fence.

Familiarize yourself with local bike-parking rules and avoid locking to anything that has been expressly marked as off-limits. In New Orleans, all of the aforementioned options are acceptable bike-hitching posts, but this may not be the case where you live. In New York, for instance, it is illegal to lock up to trees and to railings near subway stops, while Minneapolis bans locking bikes to streetlamps, parking meters and fences.

When parking on a sidewalk, leave as much room as possible for pedestrians to pass and make sure your bike isn't jutting out into a travel lane or a parking lane. Although it should go without saying, be sure to avoid spots such as handicapped ramps and locking up in a way that blocks access to a commercial entity or residence. Finally, when possible, park your bike in a well-lit, high-traffic area where someone would have to be especially brazen to try to take off with it.

IN CASE OF THEFT

Ultimately, no matter how carefully you lock your bike, there is no guarantee against bike theft. In New Orleans, the skeletal remnants of bicycles lying forlornly on their sides next to bike racks and street signs are a fairly common scene. Saddle, wheels, handlebars, and sometimes even chain have been stripped and carried away, while the lock remains securely in place.

If your bike is stolen, call your local police department's non-emergency number to file a report. Having a strong description and photos of your bike can help in getting it back or in filing a claim with your insurance company. Registering your bike with the local police department is also a good idea and costs only a nominal fee. In many cities, including New Orleans, registering your bike is required by law. Many bike shops will take care of registering your new bike for you.

{a properly locked bike—around the frame and a pole secured to the ground and through the wheel}

Beads, Booze, & Bikes:
Mardi Gras & Rethinking the Meaning of the Street

"The notion that streets are for people is a very powerful concept." -Janette Sadik-Khan, *former New York City transportation commissioner*[162]

"So shake your tambourine
Like they do down in New Orleans
A big time serenade
We going to a street parade
And we gonna second line
We gonna have a good time, time, time"
-Earl King, Street Parade

I sit down to write this the morning after the close of yet another Carnival season, a time when most people across New Orleans are pulling themselves out of bed still hazy with the fog that is the result of weeks of far too much alcohol and sugar and far too little sleep. They glint with the glitter of unknown provenance found in hair, nostrils, ears, that will continue, along with downy, brightly hued feathers, to be found in cracks and crevices, in clothing, and in bed sheets for months to come. Many of us step over wigs, wings, and tutus that have yet to be stuffed back into the costume box, that staple of New Orleans households, and finish off the remaining shreds of stale king cake left by a neighbor on the kitchen counter. There is a certain relief in the recognition that this is the last of the only-moderately-tasty-yet-impossible-to-resist-sugar-encrusted pastry that will tempt with its sprinkles of purple, green, and gold until next year, even as the rest of the day is—for most of us—a lesson in the flip side of euphoria, a steep descent on the happiness rollercoaster that has been climbing for weeks. It is, quite possibly, the least productive day of the year.

Despite its reputation as an alcohol-fueled striptease, Mardi Gras is an increasingly rare intergenerational celebration commemorated in countless ways across the city, well beyond the bounds of Bourbon Street. Although it may not be clear to those living outside South Louisiana or Mobile or Brazil, Carnival season is a not limited to a single day. Rather, it is a weeks-long celebratory period beginning January 6th and culminating on Mardi Gras Day, which is, for observant Catholics anyway, the last hurrah before Ash Wednesday and the onset of Lent.

Certainly, there is alcohol involved. And sometimes there is nudity. But Carnival season is also spending weeks constructing clever costumes. It's families coming together for parade parties and open houses. It's camping overnight to secure spots along the parade route and hosting extravagant tailgates on neutral grounds lined with Port-o-Johns, stereo systems, and complete sets of living room furniture. It is, on one end of the spectrum, balls hosted by the city's financial upper crust who, with little hint of irony, name kings and queens, dukes and maids, and parade around hotel ballrooms adorned in jewels and costumes that rival those of the Royal Family. On the other extreme, it is inner city black men who spend all year constructing resplendent feather-and-bead-costumes debuted with their Indian tribes on Mardi Gras Day, spy boys and flag boys and big chiefs, in homage to the role native Americans played in aiding ancestors' escape from slavery. It is astringent satire, poking fun at the many deserving politicians and other newsmakers with whom locals have an axe to grind. (In the wake of Hurricane Katrina in 2005, the U.S. Army Corps of Engineers has been a perennial favorite.) It is trees coated in shimmering strands of beads that hang down like colorful Spanish moss. It is grown women and men tripping over one another to catch painted shoes and coconuts tossed from floats that will be prominently displayed on mantelpieces for years to come. It is more music in the streets and the clubs than any one person can realistically take in. And, amid the bead-infused bacchanalia, it is people walking, biking and rolling around at a frequency I would hazard to guess surpasses any other time of year.

The rise in bicycling around Carnival time is not related to any particular citywide push or deep-seated environmental sensibility (after all, an estimated 150 tons of trash were swept away from city streets upon the closing bell of Mardi Gras 2015).[163] Rather, I would submit that the growth in pedal-powered traffic this time of year is rooted squarely in the fact that biking is, for those us who are physically capable of it, simply the fastest and least frustrating way to get around the city.

Bicycling for transportation is catching on in my city to the point where we now stand among the national leaders for the rate of people who get to work by bike. Yet even as New Orleans is home to a relatively large and growing population of bike commuters, the car remains the predominant mode of transportation. For those with access to a car, unless you're traveling to the French Quarter, to a Saints game, or to one of the city's many festivals, driving is typically the fastest and easiest way to get around town. But Mardi Gras turns the transportation-convenience paradigm on its head. As the parades start to roll and the streets fill with revelers, parking becomes scarce and expensive and automobile traffic—where it is allowed—grinds to a standstill, even miles away from parade routes.

Well before and also after a parade, the space usually dominated by cars turns into a massive, rollicking street party. People wander along the avenues looking for friends and stopping in at house parties thrown by people with whom they may have only the most tenuous of connections. Along the parade route, they play music and dance beneath the shade of the oak trees. Guys in jester hats, itinerant peddlers mostly descended from Midwestern locales for the season, hawk cotton candy and cheap plastic trinkets that will seem a mistake the next day. Face painters weave through the crowds while other self-appointed venders wander around selling beer bought at the convenience store down the street or mini pecan pies made in their kitchens that very morning, as a more collegiate set passes around Jell-o shots doled out for free in a fit of Carnival-inspired generosity. They drape picnic blankets and tarps and furniture across streetcar

tracks on St. Charles Avenue, crippling an otherwise popular transit line, and pull out vast spreads of sandwiches and cookies and king cake from oversized ice chests on wheels. Families, teenagers and senior citizens walk and bike, skateboard and rollerblade, while small children play games of catch and soccer. The scent of hamburgers and boiled crawfish and funnel cake and beer fills the air. And during this time, cars that can otherwise feel like mechanisms of freedom start to feel like hulking, expensive liabilities.

Before I discovered transportation bicycling, when I lived Uptown a block from the city's primary parade route, if I expected to need my car at any time on a parade day, I would plan ahead and park it outside "the box," so named because this territory is encompassed by parades on three sides and the Mississippi River on the other. But even if driving to work in the morning was relatively unchallenging, returning in the evening was another story. Parking is scarce on a usual basis in my old neighborhood, built before the rise of the automobile and markedly missing garages and driveways that are staples of our post-war suburbs. During the final week of Carnival season, finding a space to park near my old house after 3 p.m. was a sure sign that the universe was on my side.

In light of the parking constraints, there is a tradition wherein residents living near the parade route secure space for their vehicles by roping off sections of the public street with ladders, tables, trash cans and related ephemera pulled from their houses and tethered together with bright yellow caution tape. This at once strikingly illegal and widespread practice is mostly ignored by city officials with plenty of other things on their plate and by neighbors who benefit from similar arrangements.

Even though they don't seem especially concerned with this almost comical misappropriation of the public right of way, meter maids are out in full force, ticketing errant drivers for parking infractions that might be overlooked other times of year. Smelling opportunity, schools with parking lots sell off spaces that by the end of a busy Carnival season could serve as down payments on new library wings and research labs. This year my apartment building raffled off parking spaces normally reserved for residents on the day of the popular Endymion parade for $50 a pop.

Perhaps my favorite example of New Orleanians' parking-related entrepreneurialism comes from my father, who before the onset of health problems was an avid participant in the city's festival culture despite his residence 80 miles away in Baton Rouge. As per their then-annual tradition, my dad and three of his friends met up early on a Mardi Gras morning to make the drive to New Orleans. Typically, they got an early enough start that they were able to find parking along Esplanade Avenue, an easy walk into the French Quarter. But this particular year, one of the friends was late, and by the time the group pulled into the city there was no parking to be found anywhere close to where they were going.

After riding around for some time, they found themselves on a street rather far removed from the festivities, in a neighborhood where many of the houses were boarded up or densely covered in vines in testament to the poverty in which many in my city live. There they

came across the lone street space large enough to just barely fit the oversized Ford sedan in which they had ridden. But it was surrounded in yellow tape, with a middle-aged man standing next to it, smiling and waving at them to pull in. One of the friends rolled down a window.

"Just $20 for the whole day," the man beamed of the deal he was confident he was trading for the public street parking space in front of his house. "I'll keep watch on it for y'all. And my wife'll feed y'all when you come back."

My father and his friends returned later that evening, drained but happy after a long day of people watching, dreading the long drive back, and famished. As promised, their make-shift parking space attendant was waiting for them when they returned to the car. He darted into his house when he saw them, coming back out with folding chairs that he opened onto the sidewalk. His wife followed, carrying with her steaming plates of red beans and rice and cornbread. My dad and his friends devoured the food as the man preceded to share, as New Orleanians are apt to do with little prompting, the story of his life: his childhood in Detroit, how he ended up in the South, how he met his wife. It was the best $20 they'd spent all day, all agreed in the car as they headed back toward Baton Rouge.

Where driving and parking are difficult, people are more apt to consider alternatives.[164] It's a phenomenon that can be seen first-hand in places like New York, which boasts the highest share of non-car commuters in the nation.[165] And it is similarly evident in New Orleans certain times of year. Amid the challenges of driving and parking, many city residents—even some who never give second thought to hopping in their cars to go everywhere—opt to leave their cars at home and find other ways to get around.

"Pretty much the only time of year I ride my bike in New Orleans is Mardi Gras," said Andrea Mabry, a photographer. "The rest of the time I'm too freaked out by the crazy drivers and holey roads. But on busy parade days, and even the day before parades in my neighborhood, I try not to drive. It's a huge pain to drive, and it's so much better to ride. On a bike, you can go where cars can't. I've biked past all the floats lining up on Convention Center on my way Uptown to watch parades. I've navigated through standstill traffic with no problem while on the way to and on the way home from parades. It's faster to bike during Mardi Gras than drive and you don't have to worry about parking. And I see things I wouldn't see if I was in a car."

It's not just easier to get around by bike at Mardi Gras. For many, it feels more comfortable doing so than at other times of year. Headed to or from the large festivities, cars creep along at a snail's pace, their slow speeds allowing bicyclists to whir easily past. Amid so many more bicyclists and pedestrians in the street, many drivers' behavior and attitudes seem to shift. They navigate their vehicles more carefully, tentatively, even apologetically, amid the critical mass of people filling the streets, as though this is not space in which they belong but that they are instead borrowing. I suspect there may also be a social contagion component to the phenomenon. With so many people choosing to walk or bike to get places, the modes start to feel, even among those who may not consider them otherwise, like viable options.

Certainly, there are plenty of people who haven't yet caught on. My aunt lamented this year that she spent two hours stuck in traffic driving the mile home from a parade. I held my tongue when the woman sitting next to me in a suburban nail salon this Carnival season exclaimed to the man massaging her feet: "I just don't know how people get to the parades. There's so much traffic!"

In New Orleans, partying in the street is something of a specialty and, come to think of it, not just at Carnival time. Mine is a city where you never know when you might be driving along only to find the street blocked by a second line that comes strutting past, parasols and tubas and tambourines dancing through the air, a phenomenon the late, great Earl King captured so magically in the song Street Parade, his anthem to New Orleans' street party culture. (Google it. You won't be disappointed.) Or, because someone has just seen their great aunt's sister's cousin poke her head out of her front door and abandoned his car in the middle of the road to get out and say hello. Or, because a group of friends is walking in the middle of the street, having determined the street preferable to the nearby sidewalk buckled by tree roots and deferred maintenance. And while there are those pushing back against this very liberal interpretation of the meaning of the street in New Orleans culture, ours is a city, it has often been observed, that operates on a different clock from most of the world, where efficiency almost always takes a back seat to pleasure.[166] No time is this more evident than at Carnival season, in which people across the city, and sometimes across the entire metro region, are forced to rethink the meaning of streets and our relationship to them. Increasingly, cities across the globe are experimenting with events aimed at challenging long-engrained notions of what the streets are for.

It's hard to say with any certainty just how many people bike at Mardi Gras. Because Carnival is both spatially and temporally dispersed, it's hard enough to estimate just how many people participate, let alone how they get around. (I suspect that a dearth of research into the topic also reflects the celebratory bent that takes over even the most serious of academics this time of year.) But there are bits and pieces of evidence that support what experience suggests: that Mardi Gras is one of the most-biked times of year here.

The week before Mardi Gras is consistently one of the busiest times of year for Bicycle Michael's, a bike shop on Frenchmen Street in the Faubourg Marigny. The shop is flooded with repair requests in particular in the days leading up to Fat Tuesday, said employee Travis Johnson. "We get a lot of people with rusty bikes that haven't been ridden since last year's Mardi Gras."

Jefferson Davis Parkway (its name a regular reminder to those of us who might forget from time-to-time that New Orleans really is part of the South) is a corridor well-used by bicyclists and pedestrians alike thanks to the multi-use path running along its median that connects across Interstate 10, linking Mid City neighborhoods with those running along the Mississippi River. Because Jeff Davis is equipped with an automated foot and bike traffic counter, it also provides some insight into the trends in bicycling activity throughout the year.

Jeff Davis is a near-direct conveyance for pedestrians and bicyclists to the Endymion parade, one of the largest and purportedly best-attended of Mardi Gras and the only parade to roll through Mid City. In 2014, on the day of Endymion, the counter logged 3,388 foot and bike trips, a 409 percent increase over the average daily total of 665.[167] [168]. Although the equipment installed at the time didn't distinguish between bicyclists and pedestrians, in 2015, a new counter system registered a slightly higher tally for parade, with 3,432 total users recorded, 2,436 of them on bikes.[169]

"We sort of default to the automobile as the only thing that can happen in the streets," Gabe Klein, a former commissioner of Chicago's department of transportation, observed in a film about the rise of so-called open streets celebrations around the globe. These are periodic events in which streets are shut down to car traffic allowing people to roam freely where automobiles usually dominate. "The reality is that if you look back to the turn of the last century," Klein said, "there weren't any automobiles and it was people using the streets on streetcars, people on horses, people on bicycles and people walking in the streets."[170]

Bogota, Columbia is generally credited with having given rise to the open streets movement in the 1970s. As part of what Bogota has dubbed its Ciclovia, literally translated as "bicycle way," according to my Mexican stepmother, every Sunday, more than 70 miles of Bogota streets, including 7th Street, one of the main commercial corridors, are shut down to all but foot and bike traffic. The event draws an estimated two million people out into space normally choked with automobiles and exhaust.[171]

The streets, as journalist Mike Power described of one particular Ciclovia Sunday, "are filled with elderly strollers in superfly shades carrying massive radios listening to tango, children scrambling round on toy bikes, punks on skates, stern-faced Lycra warriors on $5,000 Treks, moody Goth skateboarders and, fabulously, one man and his pitbull in matching leather harnesses, panting in unison."[172]

The concept has spread rapidly. By one estimate, there are more than 400 such events taking place around the globe.[173] In North America, more than 90 open streets events are now held in places as disparate as Brownsville, Texas, Atlanta, Georgia, and Madison, Wisconsin.[174] Cities including Jakarta and Tel Aviv have adopted their own brand of Ciclovia, London's mayor is considering banning cars on Sundays, and in the City of Lights, Paris Plage, so-named for the sand and palm trees that are trucked in to fill a half-mile stretch of the quais along the Seine, render that space off-limits to cars from July to August.[175][176] New Orleans, too, I should mention, has tried to follow suit, though the only official open streets event held to-date was fraught with delays and planning challenges and wasn't especially well-understood or attended, despite organizers' laudable efforts. Perhaps they should have called it Mardi Gras.

As I've already mentioned, Mardi Gras isn't the only time when people in my city take to two wheels en masse. We are a people that live for celebration and will throw a festival for just about any reason, so long as there is music, dancing, and food involved. Festivals celebrating the po-boy, mirliton, zydeco, gumbo, Louis Armstrong, the cocktail, and the Creole tomato are among the long and varied list of events held in my city. There are so many festivals in New Orleans and its environs that for a time a local woman made a business of creating an annual fairs and festivals calendar, giving regular updates on weekend happenings on local radio station WWOZ.

Just about every one of these events draws people arriving on bikes in droves amid limited parking, more leisurely personal schedules, and no one worrying too much about getting sweaty en route, considering the venue, though I'm sure it also helps that our festivals tend to coincide with the nicest weather of the year. In 2014, the only time the Jeff Davis path saw more foot and bike traffic than during the Endymion parade was for the Bayou Boogaloo, a three-day music festival held along the banks of Bayou St. John immediately adjacent to the facility.[177] (In terms of ranking walking and biking, however, it's important to keep in mind that the Endymion parade was just one of many during the weeks of Carnival season and one of several taking place elsewhere on the city the same day, to say nothing of the various other ways people were celebrating.[178])

Few places are as festival-happy as New Orleans, but I imagine that almost every city has some type of event, be it a football game, county fair, or farmer's market, that could similarly be used to

entice people to experiment with active transportation. Even if it's only one day a year, biking to events such as these can provide an easy excuse to get into the saddle, even for people not yet comfortable biking to work, helping them to gain confidence and realize new possibilities for how they interact with their surroundings, and exposing them to the benefits and challenges associated with bicycling around a city. I would go so far as to say that the opportunities discovered by virtue of Mardi Gras and our other festivals are among the forces that have helped spur New Orleans' embrace of two-wheeled transportation. (The few studies that exist on the topic support the idea that large-scale events that encourage biking and walking can help to stoke a city's active transportation culture.[179]) Mardi Gras and, later in the Spring, the New Orleans Jazz and Heritage Festival, probably the second largest event in the city after Carnival, attracting an estimated 435,000 people in 2014, were the gateways to my bicycling habit.[180]

This past Mardi Gras Day, my husband Beaux, my friend Meredith, and I gathered before 8 a.m. Beaux and I sorted through our varied costume collection looking for a combination that would carry the added benefit of insulating us against the cold given the near-freezing temperatures that were unusual for a Mardi Gras Day. I donned an old mumu that I coupled with a flowing cardigan and several layers of tights, while my husband stuffed a pillow under his shirt, shaved his facial hair into a mustache, and was transformed for the day into his favorite literary anti-hero, John Kennedy Toole's Ingatius J. Reilly. Meredith, having arrived in a long purple wig draped against her porcelain skin, resembling a punk baby doll, poured some champagne into a sippy cup while Beaux stuffed a six pack into his pannier, and with that we hopped onto our bikes en route to the Faubourg Marigny, the neighborhood that for the past several years has been the inaugural point of my Fat Tuesday itinerary. We didn't make it a block before we happened across the first of many costumed bicyclists of the day, exchanging happy greetings as we passed. A couple miles later, we arrived at our friend Catherine and Gabe's house for breakfast, admiring the menagerie into which Gabe had transformed his family—giraffe, frog, panda, pelican, crab—via elaborate cardboard headpieces.

Next we all headed down to the corner of Royal Street and Franklin Avenue where hundreds had already amassed at the unofficial starting point of the Society of St. Anne Parade, a loosely-affiliated walking group that would later wend its way through the French Quarter but for now filled an entire city block with an assorted band of revelers dancing to music whose origins weren't entirely clear, smiling and laughing and spreading cheer and glitter like pixie dust. There were giant cockroaches and mutant shrimp, men and women in drag, political puns and sexualized priests, and more than a few costumed babies swaddled like mummies to a parent's chest or pulled along in decorated wagons.

By noon, we had made it down to Esplanade Avenue where we watched for a while as a drunk guy resembling a cross between a clown and the Tin Man from *The Wizard of Oz* directed traffic for the occasional out-of-towner attempting to drive his car through the people-clogged street. The drunk guy would signal them forward and then jump onto their hoods, howling with laughter at the wide-eyed, terrified drivers. We grabbed lunch at a café on Jackson Square packed with costumed customers, and wandered in the streets for a while, me attempting to snap photos of some of the more interesting scenes but overwhelmed by the possibilities. Eventually, we stumbled onto a party in a spectacular Royal Street townhouse. We didn't know the owner, but happened to spot my friend standing on the balcony and she waved for us to come on up. This being sufficient grounds for joining a Mardi Gras party, we complied.

Late in the day, we headed back to where we had locked our bikes to find a trio of street musicians just starting up. We stood and listened for a while to their impressive harmonies that were incongruent with their rag tag Carnival attire. Heading in the direction of home along Esplanade Avenue, moving easily past the red line of unmoving taillights beside us, we pulled over under the Claiborne Avenue Overpass, a vestige of 1950s planning decisions that decimated Treme, one of the oldest black neighborhoods in the country. The underbelly of the Interstate 10 overpass has in the decades since its construction been reclaimed as a focal point of some of the most inimitable New Orleans traditions. On this evening, it was filled with Mardi Gras Indians flailing their feathers and headpieces like giant puffed up birds to staccato drumbeats accented by the rhythmic percussion of the cars passing over expansion joints overhead.

By the time we made our way back around the bayou near our apartment, the sky was a cataclysm of reds, oranges, and blues that melted on the water. We arrived home and collapsed onto the couch exhausted, legs and lungs filled with immense satisfaction, while many of the cars we passed on Esplanade were undoubtedly still stuck in traffic.

Biking to Mardi Gras
(OR ANY EVENT WHERE CROWDS ARE HEAVY AND PARKING IS SCARCE)

1. *Locking up on the periphery may be preferable.* At Mardi Gras and many other festivals, the crowds can be so dense as to make it hard to navigate through to your final destination on bike. It's often easiest to bike to close to where you want to go, lock up, and walk the rest of the way. Locking up away from the throngs of people can also make it easier to get home when you're ready to leave.

2. *Lock your bike carefully.* I don't have any personal experience with bike theft during Carnival, but I know people who have had bikes or component parts stolen. "The Wednesday after Mardi Gras there are lots of bikes chained to the fence at Washington Square Park," says Matt Kyte, who pedals past this spot in the Marigny neighborhood every day on his way in to work. "Quite a few have wheels missing." Learn proper bike-locking technique and employ it. Increasingly, festivals in New Orleans come with bike-parking corrals that are guarded by volunteers. Amenities like these can help to make it all the more convenient to bike since they eliminate the need to hunt for bike parking and help to ensure bikes' safety.

3. *Expect more debris in the streets and carry a repair kit.* Mardi Gras and other big events that fill the streets tend to mean more flat-inducing debris in the roads. Carry a flat-repair kit with you and know how to use it. Also, adds Chris Clark, beads strewn about in the streets can be slippery to ride over so do so with care.

4. *Your costume may interfere with your ability to ride.* In a choice between a fabulous wig or headpiece and your helmet, choose your helmet, says Tara Tolford. It's also a good idea to remove long, dangling beads that can get stuck in your spokes or handlebars before riding home, adds Jennifer Ruley. Finally, remember the importance of standing out. Many parades and festivals kick off during the daylight hours and stretch into the night. Plan accordingly by equipping your bike with good lights and carrying with you reflective gear to make yourself as visible as possible.

5. ***Know your limits.*** Almost a quarter of bike fatalities in the U.S. involve a bicyclist with a blood alcohol concentration of greater than 0.08, the legal limit for driving.[181] Although a technicality in Louisiana law as of this writing means that bicyclists in this state can't be prosecuted for drinking too much before getting into the saddle, in other states, bicyclists are regularly cited for bicycling after drinking, and it's a really bad idea to drink too much before biking no matter where you live.[182]

Cycling in the Crescent City

How New Orleans Became An Unlikely Poster Child for the Bicycling Renaissance & What This Means for the Rest of the South

"It's not New York, it's not Seattle, it's a party town."
-Elizabeth Stella, protesting the New Orleans ban on smoking in bars adopted in 2015.[183]

"When I was growing up, if you saw an adult on a bike, you either thought they stole the bike, or they were from some far-off corner of the planet like California. Now, it's almost like there are more adults on bikes than kids."
-Jodi Borello, New Orleans comedian[184]

*I*f your knowledge of Seattle is anything like mine, which is to say, shaped by stereotypes augmented by limited first-hand experience, perhaps when you think of the place you too imagine a stunningly beautiful city that is home to a sea of coffee houses, legalized marijuana, and left-leaning progressive types. These are the types of people for whom GMO regularly bubbles up into everyday conversation, who carry REI frequent-buyer cards in their wallets, and who dress as though they own stock in North Face and Patagonia. They have their radios perpetually tuned to NPR, go hiking and camping on the weekends, and cart their groceries home—in reusable grocery bags of course; they don't have plastic bags at the grocery store—by foot or by bike, using their spectacularly-toned gluteal muscles to propel them, or if their families are large or their loads especially bulky, in the backs of their Subaru Outbacks, which might as well be the city's official motorized vehicle. In short, based on my trips there for a week or so at a time to visit my mother, who has taken to the place as a summertime refuge from the sweltering subtropics, and the two sets of sisters-and-brothers-in law who live there year-round, they are people who think and act an awful lot like me.

This caricature is not at all intended to disparage Seattle. In addition to being a beautiful place, it is also a tremendously well-functioning city filled with smart, ambitious, lovely people, including several of my very own friends and family members, most of whom fall squarely into the aforementioned typology. (Upon being asked on a trip home if she would ever move back to Louisiana, one of my sisters-in-law, a midwife and doctor of naturopathic medicine, a profession that I'm not even sure exists where I live, remarked in all earnestness, "I just don't know what I would do if I found out they gave my son Cheetos at school.") Rather, I make these observations here because they help to explain the collective shock felt by those of us who pay attention to such things upon hearing the 2013 bike-commute survey results announced by the U.S. Census Bureau's American Community Survey. The ACS is one of the primary mechanisms used to gauge how many people are getting around by particular modes of transportation by city.

New Orleans—our funky, strange, more-than-a-little-dysfunctional, and utterly inimitable city, a place where fried dough soaked in powdered sugar represents part of our signature fare, where you can pick up a daiquiri from the drive-through lane, where we lob boat loads of plastic beads made in China from our floats at Mardi Gras, and where plastic bags are still found in plentiful supply in our grocery stores (as my Seattleite brother-in-law pointed out distastefully last time he visited)—had a higher proportion of residents pedaling around in 2013 than ever before, when the share of people commuting by bike reached 3.6 percent.[185]

This number would have been noteworthy enough on its own at a time when the national bike-commute rate lingered below one percent, and for the change the figure represented—an astonishing 208 percent increase over year-2000 figures.[186] But even more remarkable to my mind was the company this auspicious number placed us in. New Orleans had risen above Seattle (Seattle!) in the rate of people commuting by bike. We had bested The Emerald City by just one-tenth of one percent, but this fraction felt (admittedly to a rather small fraction of us) about as significant as the time Garrett Hartley made the 40-yard field goal that secured our beloved but perennially beleaguered Saints football franchise a spot in the 2009 Superbowl. It was yet another reminder that times, they are a changing.

Increasingly, the ACS and various other measures suggest what most people have observed if only through their car windshields—that transportation bicycling is on the rise across the country, and especially in large urban areas. It is not, however, catching on in equal measures. And there is one geographic region that is lagging quite blatantly behind.

Bike commuting in the South stood at roughly half the national average as of the 2008-2012 ACS, with just 0.3 percent of southerners getting to work by bike.[187] Of the five states with bicycle commuting rates lower than 0.2 percent—Alabama, Arkansas, Mississippi, Tennessee, and West Virginia—all of them fall below the Mason-Dixon line.[188] Just three of the nation's 70 largest cities that made it to the League of American Bicyclists' Top 20 list for bike commuting in 2013 were southern. These were Washington, D.C., whose bike-commute rate of 4.5 percent was second only to that of Portland (that beacon of bike friendliness among large American cities); Austin, whose 1.4 percent bike-commute share was barely enough to qualify for the Top 20 in an increasingly competitive field; and New Orleans.[189]

Incidentally, these are each cities in which I have lived. To my surprise, I realize as I write this, apart from Washington, D.C., New Orleans is the most-biked place of the five U.S. cities I have called home, though when I lived in the nation's capital in the late 90s and again in the early 2000s, it wasn't nearly the bicyclists' paradise it is today. The 2000 Census found the District's share of residents bicycling to work that year was only around 1.1 percent, slightly below that of New Orleans at the time.[190]

As with most things involving human behavior, the South's slower embrace of two-wheeled transportation is the result of the interplay of a complicated knot of factors that are hard to disentangle. Even so, I think the essence of this phenomenon can be summed up in two major elements: early-to- mid-20th century planning decisions that prioritized cars over people, and, relatedly, I would argue, cultural resistance to a practice that is anathema to many southerners.

I should mention here what many have proffered as a third major impediment to cycling in the South: the infamous heat and humidity that have their grips on us for a good part of the year. Some very thoughtful researchers have posited that heat concerns here may be a driving force in sluggish rates of transportation bicycling.[191] To these researchers I would ask, "Have you ever visited New Orleans in August?" While I'm certain that the heat does turn many people off and that showers at more workplaces would help to make the practice more appealing, I'm not at all convinced that climate is a foremost reason for southerners' cycling abstinence. After all, people elsewhere in the country bicycle through all types of weather extremes, and for a good three-quarters of the year in much of the South, the temperatures are actually quite pleasant. "In Colorado we have winter and snow to deal with," says my friend Lee Carter, who lives outside of Boulder where a staggering eleven percent of workers bike to their jobs.[192]

The South exploded in the post World War II era, when the prospect of plentiful land, economic opportunity, and air conditioning technology newly available to the masses made living in sweltering climates imminently more bearable and helped to pull people South in droves. ("The suburban American dream," Rebecca Rosen wrote succinctly in *The Atlantic* on this subject, "was built on the sweat of air conditioners."[193]) Over the course of the 20th century, the U.S. population shifted South and West. These regions experienced the majority of the country's population growth in this period, especially in the second half of the century.[194] In 1950, the proportion of the American populace living in the Sun Belt was 28 percent. Fifty years later, 40 percent of this country's residents called the Sun Belt home.[195]

Taking place amid a sharp rise in personal car ownership, this rapid explosion in Sun Belt cities was built around the sprawling, low-density, suburban-style development patterns that have been described in more detail in an earlier chapter of this book. Even as our highway-building frenzy has slowed, many cities in the South have subsequently been slower to adopt bicycle-supportive infrastructure and policies than those in other regions of the country. (There are, of course, some notable exceptions.[196] I remember visiting my friend Mark in Nashville in 2007 and staring out the window on the drive to his house from the airport at the white striping that lined many of the roadways. "Those are bike lanes," he saw fit to inform me. New Orleans wouldn't get its first bike lane until the following year.)

Bike facilities are built when the public and the policy makers demand them. When your public —the most vocal contingent of your public anyway—is accustomed to hopping into cars to get where they need to go, they aren't likely to recognize the value of accommodating other modes of transportation. The same holds true for the people designing our roads.

I recently sat through a day-long gathering of southern traffic engineers at which a longtime member of the industry group gave a presentation that centered on his recent trip to Venice, Italy. He talked for half an hour, marveling at the efficiency of that city's transit system and how virtually everyone walked and biked to get places. "They don't allow cars within city limits!" he exclaimed. When he asked if anyone had any questions, I raised my hand, inquiring whether there were any transportation takeaways he picked up in Venice that he thought might be applicable in a city like New Orleans. He thought for a few seconds before responding. "Not really," he shrugged.

New Orleans is usually a reliably-eccentric counterpoint to national trends, and, for that matter, to most southern ones. As any New Orleanian will proudly tell you, this city is far more Caribbean in its ethos than either American or southern, a bohemian outpost that despite its geographic constitution doesn't fully belong to anyplace but itself. (Witness, among countless other examples, Ruthie the Duck Girl, who requires many more words than I can manage here, our above-ground cities of the dead, and among other unusually lax, by American standards at least and certainly by southern ones, attitudes toward alcohol, nudity, and general flamboyance.) Thus, it is all the more remarkable that we find ourselves fully entrenched—and in some ways even in the vanguard—in the two-wheeled transportation revolution sweeping the nation.[197]

Some of the forces that have conspired to make New Orleans a rather unlikely poster child for cycling are similar to the pressures at work elsewhere in this country and around the world, including growing concern for the environmental implications of fossil fuel-based transportation; the expansion of bike-friendly policies, programs, and infrastructure; and recognition of health and fitness, economic, and equity benefits of bicycling. All of these justifications are now routinely touted by public officials as they cut ribbons on new bike lanes and related infrastructure around the city.[198]

Whereas New Orleans was home to eleven miles of bikeways in 2005, as I write this in early 2015, city officials proudly boast of 95 miles, a tally that is expected to soon cross the 100-mile mark.[199] This expansion is in keeping with "complete streets" legislation adopted by the City Council in 2011 that requires that accommodations for all users—including bicyclists, pedestrians, and transit riders—be considered in designing city street projects.[200]

New Orleans' steady growth in bicycling facilities and bicyclists is even stirring our own local brand of "bikelash," as evidenced by a lawsuit brought against the city by a group of business owners trying to stop a proposed street reconfiguration in the Central Business District that would restrict automobile traffic to one lane and remove some on-street parking to accommodate a bike lane. The city moved ahead anyway.[201]

Bicycle facilities appear to be making a big difference in New Orleans in enticing people to take to two wheels. Tulane University researchers found that after the installation of the city's first on-street bike lane along St. Claude Avenue in 2008, average daily bicycle ridership there had increased 57 percent just six months after the lane's installation. The rise was especially pronounced among female riders whose ranks grew by 133 percent, compared with just 44 percent among males, an indication, the researchers concluded, of the importance of dedicated bicycle facilities in encouraging women in particular to feel comfortable hopping into the saddle.[202]

Similarly, University of New Orleans researchers have noted a continued increase in average daily bicycle traffic since they began counting bicyclists at various points across the city in 2010, with the change especially pronounced at sites that are equipped with bicycle facilities or that lie adjacent to such facilities.[203]

Although bicyclists are legally allowed on almost every street, a bike lane, even in the form of some simple striping that doesn't provide any physical protection from motor vehicle traffic, presents a loud, clear message to everyone using the road that "bikes belong here." In this way, even the most basic of bike lanes make me and a lot of other people I know feel far more comfortable riding on roads where facilities like these exist.

Esplanade Avenue provides a case in point of the value of dedicated bike facilities. Until a recent redesign, the avenue's four narrow travel lanes (designed at a time when the object was to move as much traffic as possible as quickly as possible through the corridor) resulted in "white knuckled rides" for bicyclists and motorists alike.[204] In 2013, as part of a repaving project, the two narrow lanes were converted to one, making room for a bike lane, wheelchair-accessible curb ramps, and more space for parking.

This so-called "road diet," one of the first in the city at the time, was not without its detractors, some of whom crowded into public meetings on the project prophesying massive traffic jams and other apocalyptic outcomes. But the naysayers' dire predictions never came to fruition. Instead, this tree-lined thoroughfare stretching between New Orleans' City Park on one end and the French Quarter on the other, has been recreated, to my mind and many others,' as one of the most pleasant to navigate in the city regardless of travel mode.

Bicycle ridership along the avenue has grown consistently over the past several years, according to counts conducted by the UNO Pedestrian and Bicycle Research Center, and particularly in light of the new bike facilities. Between 2013, when the bike lanes were installed, and 2014, the last year for which there was information available, bicycle ridership grew by more than 45 percent.[205] As of the 2014 data, Esplanade Avenue also had the highest proportion of female riders of any count site in the city: around 43 percent.[206]

The rather swift and recent rise of bicycling in New Orleans owes itself at least in part to one of the nation's most terrible disasters. The city's bike-lane-building bonanza began rather unceremoniously in the wake of Hurricane Katrina, when New Orleans benefited from an influx of federal recovery dollars to help rebuild its streets. Bike lanes and related infrastructure had been the mostly-unheeded rallying cry of a committed group of bicycle advocates for years. The storm rebuilding process—specifically the mass reconstruction of city streets—provided a prime opportunity to get some of these plans implemented.[207]

The storm also brought in its aftermath a surge of young idealists, many of them hailing from other locales with strong cycling traditions. They are among those adding to the ranks of Bike Easy, the local advocacy organization, and showing up at public meetings and calling their council members to lobby in favor of the city's pro-bicycle plans.[208]

Yet New Orleans' cycling ranks are not exclusively built on "young, strapping, fit people," as my friend and fellow urban planner Peter Bennett puts it. Rather, many bicyclists here are members of the city's poor and carless populations and have long gotten around by bike out of necessity. Today, we are a city that is whiter and wealthier than before the storm, but New Orleans remains majority black and disproportionately poor.[209] Car ownership has risen since Katrina, but the share of New Orleans households without access to a car is more than double the national figure.[210]

Even before Katrina and any bike lanes were built, New Orleans had certain inherent advantages that made bicycling something of a natural fit for the city. Unlike many American cities, and certainly unlike the Atlantas and the Dallases and the Houstons of the world, much of New Orleans developed prior to the rise of the personal automobile. The city rose up initially around pedestrians and horse and buggy in the Vieux Carre, the city's original settlement, and later, around the streetcars that spurred the creation of neighborhoods we know today as Uptown and the Garden District.

Although most of the streetcar network was dismantled by the 1950s and is only now gradually being pieced back together again, and while we most definitely have some textbook examples of suburban-style development (certainly in our suburbs but even within city limits) New Orleans remains a relatively compact city of well-connected, gridded streets, and a strong integration of residential and commercial uses that can make it easier to get where one needs to go by bike. The city's flat terrain is also advantageous for bicycling, even if the steamy, rainy weather can sometimes prove challenging.

In some ways, New Orleans' suitability to bicycling owes itself to the city's failure to keep pace with the rest of the nation where population growth and economic development are concerned. New Orleans hasn't in recent times faced the same population pressures that helped spur the sprawling landscapes that characterize some of our southern neighbors in particular.

While much of the Sun Belt exploded in population starting in the 1960s, serious economic, social, and environmental problems across the state have paradoxically helped to insulate New Orleans from some of the growing pains experienced by our more economically-successful peers. Until Hurricane Katrina in 2005, New Orleans was hemorrhaging jobs and population. The city's population peaked in 1960 at 627,525. By 2005, New Orleans had lost 170,000 residents.[211] From the 1980s to the 2000s, New Orleans ranked as "the Sun Belt's premier shrinking city," in the words of noted geographer Richard Campanella.[212] Today, we are a city of 378,000 people that once accommodated almost double that amount.

Projects such as the Lafitte Greenway, a long-in-the-planning biking and pedestrian path being constructed along former railroad right-of-way and nearing completion as I write this, are possible

in significant part because New Orleans hasn't in recent history experienced the type of development pressures faced by many of its peers. An undeveloped, three-mile stretch of contiguous land such as that serving as the foundation of the greenway would be unheard of in some more economically-thriving communities.[213] Similarly, it is easier to justify reclaiming some right-of-way along multi-lane roadways for modes other than cars when the traffic counts show those roads to be overbuilt.

I asked a group of friends who live in the South why it is that we southerners don't bike more. As expected, the question elicited a range of responses, from tirades about the poor quality of our roads to laments about the poor skills of our drivers. "The South," said my friend Tom, "is a driving culture. This culture is exemplified in the treatment of cyclists, the conditions in which cyclists ride, and the mentality of city planners." To this, Dan (a native of Philadelphia who has spent a decade in the South, where he now works in bicycle advocacy), added in a nod to the regional attitudinal difference he's encountered in his adopted home: "Hippies and tree huggers ride bikes."

While infrastructure is certainly vital in helping to influence our behavior, so, too, are more elusive cultural pressures. "In Portland, bicycling is cool," said my friend Miles. "In Birmingham, not so much." And I think he's on to something.

As Portland-based researchers Jennifer Dill and Kim Voros have concluded, the bicycling behavior of the people we live, work, and play with exerts substantial influence over our own bicycling-related interests and habits. If a place is teeming with cyclists, bicycling may be more readily perceived as viable, safe and socially-acceptable.[214] In places where little bicycling occurs, the opposite perception likely holds true.

On a trip to Houston a few years back, I was impressed by the bike share kiosks set up around town, but only felt comfortable using one of the bikes on the well-protected greenway running along a bayou downtown. Over my four days in the city, I didn't encounter a single bike lane, and the few transportation bicyclists I noticed improvised bikeways using sidewalks and parking lots to avoid sprawling, high-traffic roadways. I had to laugh at the signs I came across on a popular running and walking path around Rice University that cautioned pedestrians to watch out for cars. (There were no parallel warnings, I noted, for the automobile-bound constituency.) I found the signs a perfect—if unintended—metaphor for the city, and a reminder of the way that the shape of our physical environments both reflect and define our values.

In 2011, I traveled to Madison, Wisconsin for an urban planning conference. It was my first time to the city, and, as is not unusual with these types of events, I found myself far less interested in the content found inside the conference hall than the happenings outside. Specifically, I was entranced by the city's very conspicuous bicycling culture. As I wrote on the subject upon my return home, "Bicycles, and their trappings, were everywhere in Madison."[215]

> They filled stalls outside nearly every civic and commercial venue. They whirred past the sidewalk café where I was having dinner. They included the uniform, basket-bearing cherry red variety that make up the city's new bike share program, and its more utilitarian predecessor, doused unevenly in red paint and rentable from the local library. They appeared in stickers affixed to windows of restaurants and shops, advertising cyclist discounts, and in racks fixed to the back of the city's hybrid taxi fleet. They glinted, haloed by an exuberant streetlight, in a row lining the parking lot at a popular bar as I pulled up on my rent-a-bike late on a Saturday night, making conspicuous the lone car at a venue that was packed with people.

Sure, Madison had supportive infrastructure and policies in place, thanks in part to the efforts of people like the then-mayor of the city, who at one point in the conference waddled onto the stage to address the crowd mid-way through a bike ride, his awkward stride the consequence of the bike clips he hadn't bothered removing. But what struck me most about that experience was the recognition that creating a bike-friendly city isn't just about building bike facilities (though, as New Orleans has witnessed first-hand, these can certainly be hugely important in helping to shape behavior). Instead, it's simultaneously about changing habits. And while habits have a reputation as tough things to crack, as I thought about my experience in Madison, it struck me that New Orleans is a prime example of just how malleable even seemingly intractable behavior and attitudes can actually be.

To be certain, New Orleans has a long way to go and plenty of challenges standing in the way to becoming a true bicyclists' paradise (our pothole-cratered streets and a backlog of infrastructure demands, a crime problem that makes the national news with regularity, an improving-but-still-remedial-at-best-understanding among many drivers and bicyclists as to the rules of the road, and our ever-expanding-but-still-disconnected bicycle facility network, among others). But I think my city should serve as inspiration for other cities, and in particular other southern cities, that haven't had a tradition of cycling stamped into their collective consciousness for decades.

I'm heartened by the changes already underway even in some of the most car-oriented cultures of the South. Southern cities like Memphis, Atlanta, and even Houston are witnessing some of the fastest growth in transportation bicycling in the country.[216]

As I write this, Baton Rouge, my sprawling, traffic-clogged hometown, recently adopted a complete streets policy, is in the midst of building a new greenway, and is enacting its first road diet along a major thoroughfare to better accommodate bicyclists and pedestrians.[217] [218] [219] In Dallas, where I attended high school in the 90s, I was occasionally stopped and asked if I needed help by Good Samaritans who saw me walking down the street, so unfathomable it was at the time that anyone would get anywhere willingly by any means other than driving, a new "bike czar" with Portland and Austin roots has been hired to help the city rethink its transportation strategy.[220] Memphis, along with Dallas in very recent history labeled among the worst places in the country for bicycling, has gone from a place of virtually no bike infrastructure to a projected 120 miles of dedicated bike lanes by 2016.[221] [222] In Brownsville, Texas, the southernmost tip of the continental U.S.A. where one in three residents is diabetic, 80 percent are overweight, and more than 40 percent live below the poverty line, city and public health leaders have used health and equity arguments to push through a complete streets resolution, sidewalk requirements, a safe passing ordinance, and bike parking guidelines, among other impressive measures that are helping to promote bicycling and walking and improving health and economic outcomes.[223] Houston is in the midst of building its first protected bike lane right through the middle of its downtown.[224] Meantime, right next door to New Orleans, Jefferson Parish offers one of the latest signs that the South is (slowly, at times, but surely) hopping on the bicycling bandwagon. The sprawling suburb of shopping malls, vast highways, and nearly non-existent accommodations for anyone not behind the wheel of an automobile has adopted an ambitious bicycle plan that maps the way for 460 miles of bikeways, 360 percent more mileage than the Crescent City's current figure.[225]

New Orleans represents a South whose auto domination is slowly starting to give way to a more holistic approach.

Observations From Amsterdam

A Brief Dispatch From a Bicyclists' Paradise, Sent as an Email by the Author to Her Friends and Family

Dear Friends and Family,

We are having a great time in the City of Bikes. Yesterday, we walked to a bike store/coffee shop near the harbor to pick up the very inconspicuous, black Dutch-style bikes Beaux rented us for the week and to meet our tour guide for the morning, Pete Jordan. Pete is an American expat and the author of the aptly named *In the City of Bikes*, which Beaux read and I read most of. Like the book, our tour was very comprehensive and by the time it was over I was ready for a nap, food and warmer clothes and my mood showed it.

Our day with Pete made me a lot more comfortable biking here. I learned that you basically just have to kamikaze it, which is really the only way to get anywhere in this town, because if you don't, someone will pull out in front of you and it will be impossible to get anywhere.

Bikes are literally everywhere here, tethered to seemingly every lamppost, bridge railing, and the many, many bike racks to be found across the city. Outside any large venue, it looks like the bike corral at peak times at Jazz Fest. Today we explored a multi-story bike-parking garage that is so packed with bikes that city inspectors routinely come and remove those that have been left there too long.

Given the amount of competition there is for space on the road, largely thanks to all the space occupied by bicycles on them, and the fact that there aren't really (as far as I can decipher) any hard-fast rules for how you're supposed to navigate the streets, it's kind of surprising there aren't more crashes. People swerve in and out of the streets, through intersections, between cars, on what seems mostly intuition. It looks to the outsider like total chaos, yet this system, which requires paying really close attention to what's going on around you at all times, works remarkably smoothly.

Of course, there are crashes. On our first day here while we were out running, Beaux witnessed a collision between two cyclists that happened so quickly I didn't even see it. They crashed, exchanged a dirty look, then headed on their way without saying anything to one another. There are also some pretty conspicuous bike-shaped dents on some of the cars we've seen around town.

I'm still a little nervous biking through the city, but I'm getting better at it and a lot more confident. Interestingly, no one wears helmets here, apart from the tourists. And yet for the most part, everyone seems to get by just fine, including mothers and fathers with little kids piled several at a time into various contraptions attached to their bikes. Yesterday, we saw a mother biking with a little baby on the front of her bike who was so tiny the mom was holding it's head up.

At the same time, the cars don't seem to be nearly the safety concern here that they are in the U.S. For one thing, they're not nearly as commonplace as they are in the States, and many of them are these tiny two-seater types that look a bit like go carts, travel slowly through the narrow streets and don't seem as though they would inflict much harm. For another, the drivers here are extremely careful. There doesn't appear to be any three-feet rule here as there is in a growing number of American cities, but even when the cars get inches away from me, I don't feel much fear. Of course, there are also protected bike lanes everywhere that let you avoid biking alongside cars where fast-moving motor-vehicle traffic is of greatest concern. (The mopeds that are allowed to ride in the space reserved for bicycles are another story.)

In the U.S., even though I know the laws and my rights to the road as a bicyclist, there is a nagging part of my car-centric brain that sometimes feels apologetic for being there. In Amsterdam, the exact opposite is true. In the traffic hierarchy, bikes most certainly rule. The cyclists can actually be real assholes, cutting off pedestrians, running stoplights, and generally taking every opportunity to push their way through. Yet in light of my experience biking with drivers in the U.S., I kind of appreciate this. I'm wondering if I'll have a hard time readjusting upon my return home.

Pedestrians, on the other hand, seem to get the short end of the stick here. For such a people-oriented city, the sidewalks are rather narrow in many places and you constantly have to watch out to not step in front of a bicyclist. If you do, it is my sense that you stand a high likelihood of being run over by said bicyclist and probably blamed for getting in the way.

Although drivers are remarkably respectful to other road users, stopping to let pedestrians cross the street at intersections, etc., bicyclists, in general, are not. They zoom through crosswalks with pedestrians left to wait until they can sprint across the street, not unlike I feel trying to cross Prytania Street at home thanks to the cars whizzing by. I told Beaux yesterday that I feel a bit as though I'm in the Jetsons, only the shiny metal objects people are flying around on aren't spacecraft but bicycles. I have to wonder if this isn't the future for all viable cities.

One more thing and then I'll put this tome to bed: This has to be one of the healthiest cities on the planet. People are exercising constantly, from the time they are small children well into their older years. There are no guns (or at least very few) so any gun deaths make international headlines. The air is noticeably clear (especially by contrast with smog-filled Paris). There must be very few serious car crashes, one of the leading causes of death in the U.S. I'm assuming there's nationalized health care, many people live in affordable housing units in very mixed-income neighborhoods, and the food is rich, but the portions are small. (Beaux was told for the second time by a waiter today that he was ordering too much food.) The only obese people you see are tourists. One caveat to this is that, like most European countries, there's lots of cigarette smoking here, though I think even that is on the wane and probably comparable to Louisiana's smoking rate.

Anyway, I'm attaching a few pictures from the past two days. Today we hit up the Rijksmuseum, which is known for its collection of Rembrandts and Vermeers (the photo of the woman biking with her children is actually on the bike path that runs under the museum!), had brunch at a pancake house (where Beaux was told he shouldn't order all that he wanted), sat and read and wrote outside the museum, and checked out the Red Light District. Be happy there are no photographs of that scene, which was essentially Bourbon Street with pot.

Love you all,
Emilie
April 3, 2014

APPENDIX

Before-You-Ride Checklist

Before heading out on the road, you'll want to do a quick check to make sure your bike is in proper working condition so that it's less likely you'll be stranded or forced to make any unexpected and time-consuming repairs in the middle of your ride. The pneumonic ABC can help to remember the main things to look for:

- Air (Are your tires properly inflated?)
- Brakes (Are your brakes engaged and functional?)
- Chain (Is your chain taut and properly looped around the bottom bracket and derailleur?)

It's also a good idea to check to make sure that any quick-release levers or bolts attaching your wheels to your frame are tightened, and that you have:

- Functioning lights (Especially if you'll be riding at night)
- A helmet
- A lock
- Bike tools and an extra tube or patch kit
  Depending on the weather, the transportation options in your city, and your tolerance for wetness, you might also want to have handy:
- Some cash, in cash you need to take public transit
- A plastic bag or waterproof pouch to protect your cell phone and electronic devices in case of rain
- A rain jacket, poncho, or large trash bag to protect yourself in case of a storm

Bicyclists' Rules and Rights

These are compiled from the League of American Bicyclists' database, are current as of August 2014, and are applicable in the U.S. Check your state statutes and municipal code of ordinances (these are usually accessible online) or with your local bike advocacy organization for more detailed information related to bicyclist rules and rights. Remember that many jurisdictions have bicycle rules that differ somewhat from state laws.

BICYCLES ARE VEHICLES

Across much of the U.S., bicycles are considered vehicles with mostly the same rights and responsibilities of motor vehicles. This generally means that bicycles are allowed to occupy the roadway, and that bicyclists should abide by traffic laws and signals and ride in the direction of traffic.

RIDE AS FAR TO THE RIGHT AS PRACTICABLE

In most states, bicyclists are expected to ride as far to the right of an unmarked roadway as practicable where no bike lane is provided. Typically, it is acceptable for bicyclists to "take the lane," or ride in the middle of the lane, when: 1) It is unsafe to occupy the right-most portion of the roadway, because there is debris or some other obstruction located there; 2) The lane is too narrow for other vehicles to safely pass; or 3) The bicyclist is traveling at the speed of the rest of the traffic. It is also acceptable to leave the right-most section of the roadway when preparing to turn left, to avoid a right-turn lane, and when passing another vehicle.

HELMETS ARE OFTEN NOT MANDATORY, BUT ARE A REALLY GOOD IDEA

There are no statewide laws requiring bicyclists to wear helmets in the U.S., though some states do have helmet rules that apply to those under eighteen years of age and various municipalities have broader helmet requirements in place. In Louisiana, only children under twelve are required to wear helmets.

USE LIGHTS WHEN RIDING AT NIGHT

Most states require a front white headlight and rear red taillight when riding at night. Reflectors are also required by many state and local laws.

IN SOME STATES, BICYCLISTS MUST USE DESIGNATED FACILITIES WHERE PROVIDED

In some states, bicyclists are required to use dedicated bike facilities where provided adjacent to roadways carrying motor-vehicle traffic, though these types of laws are on the decline.

DRIVERS MUST MAINTAIN A SAFE DISTANCE WHEN PASSING A BICYCLIST

In every state in the U.S., drivers are required to keep a safe distance when passing a bicyclist. In a growing number of states, safe passing distance is expressly defined. In Louisiana, for example, drivers are required to leave at least three feet when passing. In some places, legal safe passing distance is even greater or varies according to speed traveled.

IN SOME PLACES, BICYCLISTS ARE GIVEN SPECIAL LEGAL PROTECTION

A handful of states now have in place vulnerable user laws. These apply to bicyclists and to other road users such as pedestrians and motorcyclists who are not encased by their vehicles. Most vulnerable road user laws currently on the books allow for larger fines or civil liability in instances where a member of this vulnerable class is injured or killed as the result of a traffic violation.

Basic Maintenance Maneuvers

INFLATING TIRES

Tools you need: A tire pump that works with the type of valve found on your inner tubes. Keeping your tires properly inflated will make your ride easier and minimize the time you spend changing or repairing inner tubes. At home, I use a floor pump to inflate my tires. It features a head with two holes that fit the two types of valves you'll find on a bike—Schrader and Presta. It also comes with a built-in pressure gauge so that I can tell without removing the head of the pump or without bending over too far whether I've inflated my tires to the recommended pressure.

Tip: The recommended pressure (PSI) for your bike tires can often be found on the sidewall of the tire.

TO AIR UP A TUBE WITH A SCHRADER VALVE

Start by removing the black plastic valve cap. With the lever on the head of the pump in the down position (usually positioned at a right angle to the head), place the appropriate hole over the valve. (On a pump with two holes, this will be the larger hole.) Press the head down firmly over the valve and adjust as necessary until you don't hear air rushing out. Pull the lever up to lock it in place and begin pumping. Once you've reached the appropriate pressure, bend the lever back to a right angle and swiftly pull it straight off of the valve.

Tube Types

Schrader valves are uniformly cylindrical, wider than their counterparts and are common to many types of pneumatic tires.

Presta valves are skinnier and generally a bit longer than Schrader valves and are the type found on most performance bikes. They are identifiable by their tapered end and the built-in nut at the tip that must be loosened before air can be injected or removed.

TO AIR UP A TUBE WITH A PRESTA VALVE

Remove the black plastic valve cap, then unscrew the built-in nut at its head, taking care not to completely remove the nut but instead unscrewing it just to the point where it's near the end of the valve. Place the head of the pump snugly over the valve (you'll use the smaller hole on a two-holed pump for this valve type) so that you don't hear air rushing out. This may

take some manipulation and practice, especially when attempting to inflate a Presta valve for the first time. Pull out the lever to lock the head in place. Once you're finished pumping, bend the lever back to a right angle, pull it off swiftly, screw the nut back into place and replace your cap.

Occasionally, you might find that in a fit of overzealous pumping you have over-inflated your tires. This can lead to hard tires and a bumpy ride, or in the worst case, a popped tube. To deflate a Schrader valve, press a small object (a key or an ink pen will work) against the inner stem of the valve. You'll hear air rushing out. Do this a little at a time until enough air has been removed. With a Presta valve, you'll simply loosen the nut and press down on the stem with your finger to release air.

ADJUSTING SADDLE HEIGHT

Tools you'll need: if you have a quick release mechanism on your seatpost, none. Otherwise, you'll need a hex or an Allen wrench to loosen the bolt that holds the seatpost in place.

You'll be able to tell whether your saddle is set at the appropriate height largely based on your leg position. When you're sitting in the saddle, your knee should be only slightly bent when you push the pedal to its furthest extension nearest the ground. If your saddle needs adjusting, you'll raise or lower the seatpost, the bar that connects the seat to the bike. Some bikes are equipped with a quick release lever located at the base of the seatpost that allows this adjustment to be made without any tools. Otherwise, you'll need either an Allen wrench or crescent wrench to loosen the nut or the screw that keeps the seatpost in place. Loosen just as much as you need to in order to move the saddle up or down, then pull or push until the saddle is at the desired position. At this point, you'll want to tighten the bolt slightly and get on the bike to make sure the saddle is where you want it to be, then tighten the bolt a bit more to secure it.

FIXING A FLAT

Fixing a flat is among the most basic and essential repairs for anyone who rides a bike. If you care for your tires properly by keeping them inflated to the recommended pressure and steering clear of debris, you shouldn't have to deal with flats too often. But sooner or later, it is a fact of life that if you ride a bike, and certainly if you ride a bike on city streets, you will get a flat.

Flat repair was one of those rudimentary skills that I put off for longer than I would like to admit. When we first started dating, my now-husband once took a bus 80 miles to my apartment to fix the flat on my bike. I was flattered that he went to such an effort to help me, of course, but I was even more impressed that among his many other attractive qualities, he knew about bikes! Not long after that trip, he insisted on teaching me how to change a bike tube. And he found other reasons to come visit.

I bring this up in recognition of the fact that it is possible to ride your bike and avoid getting your hands greasy. If you don't have a bike-knowledgeable mate around, any bike store will happily fix your flat for you for a nominal fee.

However, one of the laws of bicycling is that you will never get a flat anywhere that is not miles away from the closest bike store, unless said bike store happens to be closed or completely out of spare tubes, your bike-knowledgeable mate is out of town, and the number on the mobile bike-repair service you recently heard about is out of service. This is from first-hand experience. For these reasons, I highly recommend learning how to do it yourself.

Fixing a flat either involves replacing the punctured tube that sits between the tire and the wheel rim with a new one or removing, patching, and replacing the tube. Taking either of these actions requires having either a spare tube or patch kit handy, along with some basic bike-maintenance tools that it's a good idea to carry with you when you ride.

Get to Know Your Brakes
Disconnecting your brakes will require slightly different protocol based on your brake type.

RIM BRAKES
These are the brake type most commonly found on bicycles. They are identifiable by their location near the tire rim, which they grip when applied to slow down and stop the wheel from moving. They typically fall into one of two categories: caliper or cantilever/v-brakes.

CALIPER BRAKES
If you have caliper brakes, open the quick release by pulling up the lever that sits just above the rubber pads.

CANTILEVER BRAKES
If you have cantilever/v-brakes, you'll squeeze the brake arms together until you are able to pop the wire out of its notch and release the mechanism.

DISC BRAKES
Once the domain of mountain bikes exclusively, these are increasingly creeping into vogue for other types of bicycles. They tend to be equipped with a quick-release mechanism, but these brakes can be very hot. Pay close attention to not touch the rotor.

REAR COASTER BRAKE
On cruisers with a rear coaster brake (those you engage by pedaling backward), you'll need a 10-millimeter wrench and a Phillips-head screwdriver to loosen and remove the assembly on the brake, which is a metal fixture attached to the chainstay.

Tools you'll need:

- A spare tube
- A pair of tire levers
- A pump that works with the type of valve found on your tube

Inner tubes come in a variety of sizes to fit different sized tires and wheels. You should be able to find the size replacement tube you need on your tire wall. Look for two numbers offset by an "x," for example, 700x32c. These numbers refer to wheel rim diameter and tire width, respectively. In buying replacement tubes, you'll match the first number (in the example above, 700), while making sure that the second number falls within the range listed on the replacement tube packaging. So if my bike requires a 700x32c tube, I might buy a replacement that is labeled as 700x23-35. You'll also need to specify which type of valve you want: Schraeder or Presta. It is important to get the correct valve for your bike so that it is compatible with the hole size in the rim.

Step 1. Remove the affected wheel from the bike frame

Disconnect the brakes on the wheel with the flat. The brakes on most bikes are found close to the wheel rims and come with a quick-release system to allow for easy disengagement. If you're having trouble with this step, you might try deflating the tire to the point that it can fit between the brake pads. See instructions on previous page.

Remove the wheel from the frame.

If your wheel is equipped with a quick-release lever on one side of the axle connecting the bike frame to the wheel, you won't need any tools to remove it. Simply lift the lever and loosen the axle nut holding your wheel in place. Otherwise, you'll need to loosen the two axle nuts holding your wheel in place using a wrench.

If you're dealing with a front wheel, you should now be able to slide the wheel off the frame. If it's a rear wheel, lift the chain off of the chain ring (you can let the chain hang) and pull the wheel off the frame. To make this easier, shift your gears to move the chain to the smallest chain ring before loosening the wheel.

Step 2. Remove the affected tube

It is the tube (which sits inside the tire and rim) that must be removed and repaired or replaced. Grab at least two tire levers.

Insert the flat end of one tire lever under the bead running along the edge of the rim. I like to insert the lever at the point on the wheel that lies directly opposite the valve stem. Be sure to get the lever under the inside edge of the tire. Bend the tire lever toward the wheel spokes and tuck the tire lever (most have hooks for this purpose) under one of the wheel spokes. This should cause the tire to begin to pull away from the rim. The space created is where you will insert the flat end of a second lever. Once you have this second lever in place, pull it around the rim in a clockwise motion (pulling the lever toward your body will help to protect your knuckles from getting

> **Tip:** Additional steps are required to remove a rear wheel on a bike with an internal hub (a small boxy device located on the rear axle that controls the gears and stands in place of a rear derailleur). On this type of bike, you'll first loosen the screw that holds the hub in place, pull the box straight off and let it hang, then loosen the nut that you find underneath. Next, you'll pull out the long straight pin that this nut holds in place (it will be covered in grease and it's a good idea to lay it down on a paper towel or something else clean and flat while you're working). Finally, loosen the axle nuts and proceed to remove the wheel as described above.

scraped by the spokes) until you have pulled one side of the tire completely off of the rim. Next, pull the valve stem out of the hole in the rim and continue pulling until you have removed the tube entirely. Now that the tube has been removed, check to ensure that the source of the flat isn't still around by carefully running your hand along the rim of your wheel and the inside of the tire.

Step 3. Insert the replacement tube.

Start by putting a little air in the replacement tube to give it some shape so that it doesn't twist while you're installing it (for instruction on pumping up a tire, see page 161). Next, insert the valve stem on the tube back through the hole in the rim, then carefully work the tube into the tire. Make sure that the tire goes in without bunching in one spot. Focus on pushing the tube into the tire, rather than worrying about getting it situated perfectly in the rim. Using both hands, and beginning close to the valve, work the tire bead (the edge of the tire) back into the rim of the wheel. Make sure that the valve is straight and perpendicular to the wheel. Pinch both sides of the tire together to make this easier. If necessary, you can use your tire lever to help in this process.

Step 4. Inflate your tire.
Make sure no parts of the tube are sticking out of the tire, then inflate the tire to its recommended pressure.

Step 5. Put your wheel back on your bike.
Reverse the steps you used to remove the wheel to reattach it to your bike, taking care that all nuts are tightened and that you re-engage your brakes. If working with a rear wheel, pull the wheel back as far back as the chain will allow, then make sure that the opposite side is pulled back to the same position. This can be a bit tricky at first. Check to be sure you've done this correctly by making sure that the hub of the back wheel is perpendicular to the bike. I like to turn the bike back over after tightening the bolts loosely

> **Tip:** Don't take the tire totally off of the wheel to fix a flat.

and spin the wheel to make sure that the repaired tire isn't rubbing on anything, which is a good sign that it's misaligned.

PATCHING A TUBE

Tools you'll need:

- A patch kit
- A tire pump

> **Tip:** In putting the rear wheel back on, you'll want to first put the chain back on the ring, then work the wheel into position.

Other uses for old tubes:

Eventually, you're likely to wind up with way more old tubes that you'll ever care to patch. In this case, you might look into recycling programs offered at some bike shops. Those that specialize in rehabbing old bikes are strong candidates. If there aren't any recycling programs in your city, check online for companies that collect and repurpose old tubes.

I've seen old tubes given new life as jewelry, Mardi Gras masks, wallets, belts, and bags. A friend of mine who likes to garden uses old bike tubes as ties for staking her tomato plants. I've also discovered in a pinch that with a simple snip, old tubes make good bungee cord alternatives.

My hall closet is a graveyard of formerly-functional inner tubes. As the months go by and the pile of serpentine black rubber strips grows ever larger, the prospect of me actually getting around to patching and reusing them seems increasingly remote. And this is unfortunate because repairing bike tubes can not only be your saving grace when you find yourself stranded without an extra inner tube: it can also save you money. Six dollars a pop for a new tube starts to add up quickly, especially if you're super flat-prone, in which case it might be worth investing in a pair of Kevlar tires to prevent punctures.

Step 1. Find the hole in your tube

If you have a pump handy, try inflating the tube a bit and feeling around for the place where air is escaping. You might also hold the tube up to your ear to see if you can hear where air is rushing out. If you can't find the hole, you can soak the tube in water and identify the problem spot by looking for the place where bubbles develop. Once you identify the location of the hole, place a finger over it while you pump up the tube a bit more. Now run your hand around the tube to make sure there aren't additional holes that may have contributed to the flat. If the hole was caused by the tube getting cinched up awkwardly (this is known as a pinch flat and is often the result of under-inflation) rather than a foreign object puncturing the tube, there may be multiple holes to attend to, often in the trademark "snake bite" configuration.

Step 2. Prime the area around the hole

Your patch kit should contain a piece of sandpaper or a metal scraper. Rub the sandpaper or scraper over and immediately around the hole until the area you are buffing loses its shine. The idea is to roughen the surface so that the patch is better able to grip the tube.

Step 3. *Adhere the patch to the tube*

Apply a layer of glue on the hole and immediately around it, roughly the same size as the patch. Allow the glue to dry for about two minutes or until it is very tacky.

If your patch kit comes with self-adhesive patches, you can skip this step, but they are generally a less reliable, temporary solution.

Step 4. *Apply the patch*

Press the patch firmly on the tube, centering it over the hole. Hold the patch in place for a minute or so, then set it aside. Wait about ten minutes, then inflate your tube to make sure the patch holds.

A Few More Helpful Maintenance Tips!
What to do when your:

CHAIN FALLS OFF

If your bike has gears, this is a fairly simple fix. Just extend the rear derailleur arm to create some slack in the chain and slip the chain back over the front chain ring.

If you ride a single speed or a bike with an internal hub, you'll need to loosen the axle nuts and move the wheel forward to create slack in the chain so that you can put it back in place.

WHEEL IS STICKING

Often, this problem stems from a misalignment of the wheel. To address it, first try loosening the axle nuts or quick release on the affected wheel and resetting it on the frame of the bike, making sure that the wheel lines up with the frame.

A sticking wheel may also mean that a brake is too tight or is turned in such a way that a brake pad is rubbing against the tire. Often, brakes can be adjusted ever so slightly without any tools by twisting them back into place.

Another possible source of rubbing or sticking is that the wheel is out of true, meaning that there is a bend in the wheel that leads it to spin unevenly. The uniform straightness of the wheel is established by a balanced amount of tension from each spoke. Wheels can be "trued" by adjusting the spokes, but this is a maneuver best left to an experienced bike mechanic.

HANDLEBARS ARE LOOSE

Find the point where the handlebars are clamped by the stem and tighten the bolt(s) you find there.

Acknowledgments

Many thanks to the folks at Microcosm Publishing, and especially Elly Blue, Joe Biel, Tim Wheeler, Taylor Hurley, and Meggyn Pomerleau, who are the reason you are reading these words. Thanks also to my dad, Len Bahr, who knew I had it in me before I did; to my mom, Carolyn Leftwich, my earliest example of a woman on bike; and to my brother, Jason Core, for re-teaching me through example that it was possible to get around on two wheels. I am forever grateful for my husband, Beaux Jones, whose patience, encouragement and agility in every type of terrain continue to amaze me, and to the many friends, family members, and strangers who shared their stories with me, pushed me to pursue this project, encouraged me with countless sources of inspiration, put up with me talking about few topics other than biking for the past few years, and who scrutinized countless iterations of the text and images contained in these pages.

In addition to those already mentioned, I am especially indebted in this regard to Stephanie Hepburn, Daisy Dodge, Andy Jacoby, Tricia Keffer, Peter Bennett, Audrey, Tricia, Vikki, and Lloyd Leftwich, Anna Foret, Catherine Markel, Stephanie Jones Jordan, Molly Jones Gray, Ammen Jordan, Elaine Guillot, Danni Jones, and Guille Novelo. Special thanks are also owed to Andrea Chen, Megan McKown, Ann Daigle, Sarah Hammett, Gwen Geletka, Paige Geletka, Lauren Bordelon, Christine Moser, Matthew Hendrickson, Jennifer Ruley, John Renne, Marin Tockman, Naomi Doerner, Mark Martin, Dan Jatres, Tara Tolford, Kate Lowe, James Wilson, Jim Amdal, Miles Granderson, Meredith Soniat, Karen Parsons, Megan Leonard, Pete Jordan, Tom Futrell, Lee Carter, George Zoeckler, Sarah al Zein, Julie Sanders, Jimmy Lopez, Paula Frederick, Jessie Eisner-Kleyle, Vivek Shah, Lord David, Chris Clark, Joel Devalcourt, Suzanna Dryden Jensen, Gabriel Markel, Matt Kyte, Rush Carter, Jamie Wine, Brooke Muntean, Dorothy Sekowski, Kelli Gilbert, Eric Peace, Angelique Panther, Kirk Hunter, and anyone else I have neglected to name.

Finally, this book owes itself to the many existing and prospective cyclists—female and male—who first prompted me to get into the saddle and to put these words to paper.

Author Bio

Emilie Bahr is a writer and urban planner living in New Orleans, where she first rediscovered the joys of getting around by bike. When she's not biking, she's often running, canoeing, or curled up in her favorite chair with a good book.

End Notes

1 Cornwall Historical Society. "Women's Rights: Cornwall's Radicals, Rebels, and Reformers." 2013.

2 Scott Neuman. "Saudi Council Reportedly Recommends Letting Some Women Drive." NPR. November 7, 2014.

3 Neuman. Saudi.

4 Bill Chappell. "Saudi Women Get Behind the Wheel for 'Drive In' Protest," NPR.org, October 26, 2013.

5 Helen Russell. "Removal of Ban on Women Cycling in Saudi Arabia is Just Gesture Politics." Metro. April 6, 2013.

6 Elliot Johnston. "Egypt Women Turn to Cycling in Fight for Equality: Feminist Movement Girls' Revolution Introduce Their We Will Ride Bikes Initiative." road.cc. November 14, 2013.

7 Jed Lepinksi. "Cycling Past An Afghani Taboo." The *New York Times*. April 16, 2013.

8 Adrienne Lafrance. "How the Bicycle Paved the Way for Women's Rights." *The Atlantic*. June 26, 2014.

9 Lafrance. How.

10 Lafrance. How.

11 "Morals of Wheelwomen; A Chicago Police Captain Thinks the Use of the Bicycle Dangerous—Mrs. Henrotin Disputes Him." The *New York Times*. May 15, 1899.

12 Johnston. Egypt.

13 Ashley Bates. "Sorry, Hamas. I'm Wearing Blue Jeans." *Mother Jones.* December 16, 2010.

14 Iyad Khuder. "Yalla Let's Bike, Let's Break the Set!" *The Newshound* Blog, December 7, 2014. Accessed February 21, 2015. http://blog. newshoundmedia.com/2014/12/yalla-lets-bike-lets-break-the-set/.

15 Janine di Giovani. "Denial is Slipping Away as War Arrives in Damascus." The *New York Times*. October 17, 2012.

16 Sarah al Zein. (In an email with the author). February 20, 2015.

17 Lepinksi. "Cycling."

18 Eben Weiss. "Don't Make Bicyclists More Visible. Make Drivers Stop Hitting Them." *The Washington Post*, April 15, 2015.

19 "Poverty." Institute for Women's Policy Research. Accessed February 14, 2015. Iwpr.org/initiatives/poverty.

20 Alyssa Sharrock. "Riding through Recovery." *Caring*, September 15, 2014.

21 Matt Flegenheimer. "Turning the City's Wheels in a New Direction." The *New York Times*, December 29, 2013.

22 Vanessa Williams. "Black Women Take Their Place in D.C.'s Bike Lanes." *The Washington Post*, July 10, 2011.

23 David Foster Wallace. "Plain Old Untrendy Troubles and Emotions." *The Guardian*, September 19, 2008.

24 Linda Baker. "Shifting Gears: To Boost Urban Cycling, Figure Out What Women Want." *Scientific American*, September 21, 2009.

25 Catherine Emond, Wei Tang, and Susan Handy. "Explaining Gender Difference In Bicycling Behavior." *Transportation Research Record: Journal Of The Transportation Research Board*, 2125 (2009): 16-25.

26 John Pucher and Ralph Buehler. "Making Cycling Irresistible: Lessons From The Netherlands, Denmark And Germany." *Transport Reviews* 28, no. 4 (2008): 495-528.

27 Pucher and Buehler. "Making"

28 Conor Reynolds, M. Anne Harris, Kay Teschke, Peter Cripton, and Megan Winters. "The Impact Of Transportation Infrastructure On Bicycling Injuries And Crashes: A Review Of The Literature." *Environmental Health* 47, no. 8 (2009).

29 Reynolds, Harris, Teschke, Cripton, and Winters. "The Impact"

30 Reynolds, Harris, Teschke, Cripton, and Winters. "The Impact"

31 Reynolds, Harris, Teschke, Cripton, and Winters. "The Impact"

32 Reynolds, Harris, Teschke, Cripton, and Winters. "The Impact"

33 Mehroz Baig. "Women In The Workforce: What Changes Have We Made." *HuffingtonPost*. December 19, 2013.

34 Reynolds, Harris, Teschke, Cripton, and Winters. "The Impact"

35 Herbie Huff and Kelcie Ralph. "The Reason Fewer US Women Cycle Than The Dutch Is Not What You Think." *The Guardian*. October 3, 2014.

36 Laura Moser. "Families Ditch Cars For Cargo Bikes," The *New York Times*, April 22, 2015.

37 Jennifer Dill and Kim Voros. "Factors Affecting Bicycling Demand: Initial Findings From The Portland Region." *Transportation Research Record: Journal Of The Transportation Research Board*, 2031 (2007): 9-17.

38 Jennifer Dill and Nathan McNeil. "Four Types Of Cyclists? Testing A Typology To Better Understand Bicycling Behavior And Potential." Portland State University. August 10, 2012.

39 Pucher and Buehler. "Making"

40 Huff and Ralph. "The Reason"

41 Huff and Ralph. "The Reason"

42 Huff and Ralph. "The Reason"

43 Ian Simpson. "FBI: Violent Crime Drops, Reaches 1970s Level." *The Chicago Tribune*, November 10, 2014.

44 Jeralynn Cossman and Nicole Rader. "Fear of Crime and Personal Vulnerability: Examining Self-Reported Health." *Sociological Spectrum*, No. 31 (2011): 141-162

45 Cossman and Rader. 2011.

46 Jeroen Johan de Hartog, Hanna Boogaard, Hans Nijland, and Gerard Hoek. "Do The Health Benefits Of Cycling Outweigh The Risks?" *Environmental Health Perspectives*, 118, no. 8 (2010): 1109-1116.

47 World Health Organization. "Physical Activity Fact Sheet No. 385." January, 2015.

48 Harvard Health Publications. "Calories Burned in 30 Minutes for People of Three Different Weights." July 1, 2004.

49 Calculation based on average weight for adult women 20 and older. Centers for Disease Control and Prevention. October, 2012.

50 Rachelle Unreich. "Catherine Baba Is A Stylist." Dumbo Feather, 2011.

51 Edward Hirsch. "Susan Sontag, The Art of Fiction, No. 143." *The Paris Review*, No. 135 (1995).

52 Carol Matlack. "NYC's Bike Sharing Makes Sense. It Probably Won't Make Money." *Bloomberg Business*, May 30, 2013.

53 Simons. "Five Years"

54 Will Coldwell. "Paris Becomes First City to Expand Bike Share to Children." *The Guardian*, June 19, 2014.

55 "Parisian Velib' Achieves Over 200 Million Rentals." JCDecaux. July 4, 2014.

56 Simons. "Five Years"

57 Ruth La Ferla. "Bicycle Chic Gains Speed." The *New York Times*. September 29, 2010.

58 Carol Glatz. "Avoid Fast Cars And Ride A Bike Instead, Pope Tells Trainee Priests and Nuns." *Catholic Herald*. July 9, 2013.

59 Kyle Stock. "Why This $11,000 Bicycle Makes Sense for Hermes." *Bloomberg Business*. October 11, 2013.

60 Natalie DiBlasio. "Retailers Rush To Tap Millennial 'Athleisure' Market." *USA Today.* December 29, 2014.

61 Ally Betker. "Heels on Wheels? Hanneli Mustaparta on How to Wear the Summer's Chicest Shoes on a Bicycle." *Vogue*, June 18, 2014.

62 Brian McKenzie. "Modes Less Traveled-Bicycling and Walking to Work in the United States: 2008-2012." American Community Survey Reports (May, 2014): 10, 11.

63 The League of American Bicyclists. "The New Majority: Pedaling Towards Equity."

64 McKenzie. "Modes." 7.

65 "Employment Status of the Civilian Population by Race, Sex, and Age," Bureau of Labor Statistics, last modified May 8, 2015, www.bls.gov/news.release/empsit.t02.htm

66 Bratman and Jadhav. "How"

67 Bratman and Jadhav. "How"

68 Veronica O. Davis, "Out of the Mouths of Babes: How a Little Black Girl Sparked a Revolution" (presentation, National Bike Summit, Washington, D.C., March 5, 2013).

69 Coldwell. "Paris"

70 Coldwell. "Paris"

71 Dill and Voros. "Factors"

72 Catherine Saint Louis. "Up The Career Ladder, Lipstick In Hand." The *New York Times*. October 12, 2011.

73 Dalton Conley and Rebecca Glauber. "Gender, Body Mass and Economic Status." National Bureau of Economic Research. May 2005.

74 Saint Louis. "Up"

75 Mikael Coville-Anderson. "Bicycle Culture By Design." TEDxZurich lecture, November 28, 2012.

76 Liz Murphy. "Bikes Mayors = A Conversation with R.T. Rybak." League of American Bicyclists. February 20, 2015.

77 Herbert Gold. "Vladimir Nabokov, The Art of Fiction, No. 40." *The Paris Review*, January 1, 1967.

78 Clive Thompson. "When Pedestrians Ruled the Streets." *Smithsonian* Magazine, December, 2014.

79 "Nation Roused Against Motor Killings." The *New York Times*, November 23, 1924.

80 "Nation Roused"

81 Thompson. "When"

82 "Nation Roused"

83 Peter Norton. *Fighting Traffic: The Dawn Of The Motor Age In The American City*. Cambridge, Massachussets: MIT Press, 2008.

84 Norton. *Fighting Traffic*

85 Peter Norton. "Street Rivals: Jaywalking and the Invention of the Motor Age Street." *Technology and Culture*, 48, No. 2 (2007): 331-359.

86 Norton. "Street Rivals"

87 Christopher Leinberger. *Futurama and the 20th Century American Dream*. In The Option of Urbanism: Investing in a New American Dream. 2nd ed. Washington, D.C.: Island Press, 2009.

88 National Center for Safe Routes to School. "How Children Get to School: School Travel Patterns from 1969 to 2009." November, 2011.

89 National Center for Safe Routes to School. "How"

90 Jonathan Nettler. "Why Suburban Sprawl Is The Worst Idea America Has Ever Had." Planetizen: The Urban Planning, Design, and Development Network. October 16, 2013.

91 Hobbs, Frank, and Nicole Stoops. "Demographic Trends in the 20th Century." U.S. Census Bureau, Census 2000 Special Reports, 2000.

92 Ada Louise Huxtable. "The Expressway Debate: Progress or Destruction?" The *New York Times*, May 1, 1967.

93 Homber Bigart. "U.S. Road Plans Periled By Rising Urban Hostility." The *New York Times*, November 13, 1967.

94 Richard Baumbach and William Borah. *The Second Battle of New Orleans: A History of the Vieux Carre Riverfront-Expressway Controversy*, 45. Tuscaloosa: University of Alabama Press, 1981.

95 William Blair. "Volpe Vetoes a Freeway to Save French Quarter in New Orleans." The *New York Times*. July 10, 1969.

96 Baumbach and Borah. xviii

97 John Pucher and John Renne. "Socioeconomics of Urban Travel: Evidence from the 2001 NHTS." Transportation Quarterly 57, No. 3 (2003): 29-77.

98 John Pucher, Ralph Buehler, and Mark Seinen. "Bicycling Renaissance in North America? An Update and Reappraisal of Cycling Trends and Policies." Transportation Research Part A 45 (2011): 451-75.

99 Pucher, Buehler, and Seinen. "Bicycling"

100 "MAP-21 Program Explainer." Transportation for America. 2013. http://t4america.org/maps-tools/map-21/ta/.

101 Andrea Milne and Maggie Melin. "Bicycling and Walking in the United States 2014 Benchmarking Report." The Alliance for Biking & Walking. 2014.

102 Milne and Melin. "Bicycling"

103 Pucher, Buehler, and Seinen. "Bicyling"

104 Pucher, Buehler, and Seinen. "Bicycling"

105 "Rails to Trails Conservancy." National and State Trail Statistics. 2015.

106 Milne and Melin. "Bicycling"

107 Colville-Andersen. "Bicycle"

108 John Pucher, Ralph Buehler, Dafna Merom, and Adrian Bauman. "Walking and Cycling in the United States, 2001-2009: Evidence from the National Household Travel Survey." American Journal of Public Health 101, Supplement 1 (2011): S310-317.

109 Pucher, Buehler, and Seinen. "Bicycling"

110 Ken McLeod. "Updated: Bike Commute Data Released." League of American Bicyclists. September 29, 2014.

111 League of American Bicyclists. "Where We Ride: An Analysis of Bicycle Commuting in American Cities." (2014). Bikeleague.org/sites/default/files/ACS_report_2014_forweb.pdf.

112 League. "Where"

113 Brian McKenzie. "Modes Less Traveled-Bicycling and Walking to Work in the United States: 2008-2012." American Community Survey Reports (May, 2014): 6.

114 People for Bikes. "U.S. Bicycling Participation Benchmarking Study Report." March 2015.

115 McKenzie. "Modes"

116 Milne and Melin. "Bicycling"

117 U.S. Census Bureau. 2009-2013 American Community Survey 5-Year Estimates. Means of Transportation to Work, Table B08301.

118 Tony Dutzik, Jeff Inglis, and Phineas Baxandall. "Millennials in Motion: Changing Travel Habits of Young Americans and the Implications for Public Policy." U.S. PIRG Education Fund and Frontier Group, October, 2014.

119 Adam Geller. "Americans' Car Ownership, Driving In Steep Decline." The Associated Press, May 31, 2014.

120 Katherine Davidson. "The End of the Road: Has the Developed World Reached 'Peak Car'?" Schroders. January 28, 2015.

121 Michael Sivak. "Has Motorization in the U.S. Peaked?" Lecture. Stanford University School of Earth, Energy & Environmental Sciences. October 20, 2014.

122 Sivak. "Has"

123 Leo Mirani. "Urbanization and Smartphones Are Killing Car Culture." *The Atlantic's CityLab*, February 2, 2015.

124 Geller. "Americans'"

125 Davidson. "The End"

126 Sivak. "Has"

127 Sivak. "Has"

128 "Millennials Prefer Cities to Suburbs, Subways to Driveways." Nielsen. March 4, 2014.

129 Nielson. "Millennials"

130 Nielson. "Millennials"

131 Dunham-Jones. "Rethinking"

132 Mark Mather, Kelvin Pollard, and Linda Jacobsen. "Reports on America: First Results from the 2010 Census." Population Reference Bureau, July, 2011.

133 William Frey. "Will This Be the Decade of Big City Growth?" Brookings Institution. May 23, 2014.

134 Frey. "Will This"

135 Frey. "Will This"

136 Joe Cortright. "Surging City Center Job Growth." CityObservatory. February, 2015.

137 Cortright. "Surging"

138 Robert McClendon. "Properties in Central City, Treme, 7th Ward, and St. Roch Draw Most Interest in Online Auction." *The Times-Picayune*, March 9, 2015.

139 McClendon. "Properties"

140 Badger. "New Census"

141 Dunham-Jones. "Rethinking"

142 Dunham-Jones. "Rethinking"

143 D'Vera Cohn. "Marriage Rate Declines and Marriage Age Rises." Pew Research Center. December 14, 2011.

144 Dunham-Jones. "Rethinking"

145 Dunham-Jones. "Rethinking"

146 As heard on the WNPR radio show "Where We Live," broadcast out of New Haven, Connecticut. February 6, 2015.

147 "U.S. Transportation Secretary Foxx Announces New Initiative to Enhance Pedestrian and Bicycle Safety." United States Department of Transportation. September 10, 2014. Dot.gov/briefing-room/us-transportation-secretary-foxx-announces-new-initiative-enhance-pedestrian-and.

148 United States Department of Transportation. "U.S. Transportation Secretary"

149 Angie Schmitt. "Anthony Foxx Challenges Mayors to Protect Pedestrians and Cyclists." StreetsblogUSA. January 23, 2015.

150 Sarah Goodyear. "As More Cities Adopt 'Vision Zero,' a Grand Experiment Emerges on U.S. Streets." *The Atlantic's CityLab*. February 20, 2015.

151 Greg Billing. "Mayor Bowser Commits to Implementing Vision Zero." Washington Area Bicyclist Association. February 26, 2015.

152 Benjamin Mueller. "25 M.P.H. Speed Limit Takes Effect in New York." The *New York Times*. November 7, 2014.

153 Joshua Sabatini. "SF examines lowering speed limits in the name of safety." *The San Francisco Examiner.* February 5, 2015.

154 Susan Dominus. "How Do We Protect New York City's Pedestrians?" The *New York Times*, April 23, 2015.

155 Tony Dutzik, Benjamin Davis, and Phineas Baxandall. Do Roads Pay For Themselves? U.S. PIRG Educaton Fund and Frontier Group, January, 2011.

156 Emma Brown and T. Reese Shapiro. "Cities Are Becoming More Affluent While Poverty Is Rising in Inner Suburbs—And That Has Implications for Schools." *The Washington Post*, February 26, 2015.

157 "Stuck in Traffic? It's Likely to Be Worse in 30 Years, Report Says." National Public Radio. February 5, 2015.

158 Adam Mann. "What's Up with That: Building Bigger Roads Actually Makes Traffic Worse." *Wired*. June 17, 2014.

159 Mann. "What's"

160 Gilles Duranton and Matthew Turner. "The Fundamental Law of Road Congestion: Evidence from U.S. Cities." National Bureau of Economic Research. Cambridge, MA. September, 2009.

161 F.H. Buckley. "We Have Not Begun to Fight the Bike Lanes." The *Wall Street Journal*, November 8, 2013.

162 Clarence Eckerson. The Rise of Open Streets. Film. January 9, 2014.

163 Janet McConnaughey. "Mardi Gras: Last Tipsy Revelers Sent Home, Trash Swept Up." *The Associated Press,* February 18, 2015.

164 Ralph Buehler. "Trends and Determinants of Cycling in the Washington, D.C. Region." Transportation Research Part D: Transport and Environment 17, no. 7 (2012): 525-31.

165 Emily Badger. "The U.S. Cities Where the Fewest Commuters Get to Work by Car." *The Atlantic's CityLab,* October 28, 2013.

166 Gary Scheets. "Permit fees raining on second-line parades." *The Times-Picayune,* March 29, 2007.

167 Tara Tolford. (University of New Orleans Transportation Institute research associate). In conversation with the author. February 12, 2015. Tally recorded March 1, 2014.

168 Tolford. Average daily trips based on June 2013-May 2014 reporting period.

169 Tolford. 2015 Endymion traffic figure based on February 14, 2015.

170 Eckerson. Rise

171 Mike Power. "Bogota's Ciclovia Could Teach Boris Johnson How to Run a Car-free Capital." *The Guardian,* June 16, 2010.

172 Power. "Bogota's"

173 "Six Ideas for Building Cycling Culture from the World Bicycle Forum." SustainableCitiesCollective. March 4, 2015.

174 Redlin. "Reinventing"

175 "London Car-free Sundays Idea to Be Reviewed, Says Mayor." *BBC News London,* November 30, 2014.

176 Eleanore Beardsley. "Sun, Sand and the Seine: The Beach Comes to Paris." National Public Radio, August 19, 2013.

177 Tolford. Bayou Boogaloo traffic was 5,442 and 5,355, respectively, on May 17th and 18th, 2014.

178 Cate Root. "Mardi Gras 2014 Parade Schedule, Day-by-day." *The Times-Picayune,* February 9, 2014.

179 John Pucher, Ralph Buehler, and Mark Seinen. "Bicycling Renaissance in North America? An Update and Reappraisal of Cycling Trends and Policies." Transportation Research Part A 45 (2011): 451-75.

180 Keith Spera. "2014 New Orleans Jazz Fest total attendance estimated at 435,000." *The Times-Picayune,* May 9, 2014.

181 "Who Is Getting Killed in Bicycling Crashes?" Pedestrian and Bicycle Information Center. Pedbikeinfo.org/data/factsheet_crash.cfm.

182 Charlie Thomas. "Lawyer Charlie Thomas Explains the Bicycle Laws of Louisiana." Bike Law. June 18, 2014. Bikelaw.com/2014/06/18/louisiana-bicycle-laws/.

183 Joanna Fantozzi. "Smoking Is Now Banned in All New Orleans Bars." The Daily Meal: All Things Food & Drink, January 23, 2015. Accessed February 6, 2015. http://www.thedailymeal.com/news/travel/smoking-now-banned-all-new-orleans-bars/012315.

184 Jodi Borello. "On the Porch with Jodi Borello: Childhood Memories That Could Only Be Made in New Orleans." *The Times-Picayune*, July 20, 2012. Accessed February 6, 2015.http://www.nola.com/family/index.ssf/2012/07/on_the_porch_with_jodi_borrell.html.

185 League of American Bicyclists. "70 Largest Cities with the Highest Share of Bicycle Commuters." September 24, 2014. Accessed February 5, 2015. Bikeleague.org/sites/default/files/ACS_report_70largest_final.pdf.

186 "Updated: Bike Commute Data Released | League of American Bicyclists." September 29, 2014. Accessed February 5, 2015. Bikeleague.org/content/updated-bike-commute-data-released.

187 Brian McKenzie. "Modes Less Traveled-Bicycling and Walking to Work in the United States: 2008-2012." American Community Survey Reports (May, 2014): 17.

188 McKenzie, "Modes Less Traveled," 7.

189 League of American Bicyclists. "70 Largest cities with the Highest Share of Bicycle Commuters."

190 U.S. Census Bureau, Census 2000, Summary File 3, Means of Transportation to Work for Workers 16 Years and Older, Table P030. Generated using American FactFinder. Accessed February 5, 2015.

191 John Pucher, Ralph Buehler, and Mark Seinen. "Bicycling Renaissance in North America? An Update and Re-appraisal of Cycling Trends and Policies." Transportation Research Part A 45 (2011): 454.

192 League of American Bicyclists. "Where We Ride: An Analysis of Bicycle Commuting in American Cities." (2014). Bikeleague.org/sites/default/files/ACS_report_2014_forweb.pdf.

193 Rebecca Rosen. "Keepin' It Cool: How the Air Conditioner Made Modern America." *The Atlantic*, July 14, 2011.

194 Frank Hobbs and Nicole Stoops. "Demographic Trends in the 20th Century." U.S. Census Bureau, Census 2000 Special Reports, 2000.

195 Rosen. "Keepin' It Cool."

196 The Alliance for Bicycling & Walking. "Bicycling and Walking in the United States 2012 Benchmarking Report."102.

197 John Pucher and Ralph Buehler. "Analysis of bicycling trends and policies in large North American cities: Lessons for New York." A report prepared for the U.S. Department of Transportation. (2011),vii.

198 Emilie Bahr. "Cycling in the Crescent City: An exploration of the spatial variation in bicycle commuting in New Orleans." (2013). University of New Orleans Theses and Dissertations.

199 Dan Jatres (pedestrian and bicycle program manager at the New Orleans Regional Planning Commission), in discussion with the author, February 7, 2015.

200 Ariella Cohen. "Cyclists and Pedestrians to Benefit from New Complete Streets Program." *The Lens.* December 28, 2011.

201 Robert McClendon. "Baronne Street Bike Lane Cleared to Move Forward; Judge Rules against Businesses." *The Times-Picayune*, November 6, 2014.

202 Kathryn Parker, Jeanette Gustat, and Janet Rice. "Installation of Bicycle Lanes and Increased Ridership in an Urban, Mixed-income Setting in New Orleans, Louisiana." *Journal of Physical Activity and Health* 8 (2011): S98-102.

203 Tara Tolford. "New Orleans 2013 Bicycle and Pedestrian Count Report." Pedestrian Bicycle Resource Initiative, Merritt C. Becker, Jr. University of New Orleans Transportation Institute. July 1, 2013.

204 Moore. Esplanade.

205 Tara Tolford (University of New Orleans Transportation Institute research assistant), in conversation with author about soon-to-be-released 2014 count data. February 12, 2015.

206 Tolford. February 12, 2015.

207 Richard Rainey. "Esplanade, City Park Avenues among Major Arteries in New Orleans Getting a Makeover," *The Times-Picayune*, March 20, 2013.

208 Campanella. "Gentrification."

209 Nihal Shrinath, Vicki Mack, and Allison Plyer. "Who Lives in New Orleans and Metro Parishes Now?" The Data Center. October 16, 2014

210 Shrinath. Who Lives in New Orleans.

211 Richard Campanella. "Gentrification and its discontents: Notes from New Orleans," *New Geography*, March 1, 2013.

212 Campanella. "Gentrification."

213 Emilie Bahr. "Some Find a Silver Lining in La. Population Decline," *New Orleans CityBusiness*, January 12, 2009.

214 Jennifer Dill and Kim Voros. "Factors Affecting Bicycling Demand: Initial Findings from the Portland Region." Transportation Researcher Record: Journal of the Transportation Research Board, 2007.

215 Emilie Bahr. "Big Easy Bike Boom." *Metropolis.* June 30, 2011. Metropolismag.com/Point-of-View/June-2011/Big-Easy-Bike-Boom/.

216 League. Where We Ride.

217 Andrea Gallo. "Metro Council Approves Policy to Make Baton Rouge More Walkable, Bike Able," *The Advocate*, November 28, 2014.

218 Diana Samuels. "Downtown Greenway to Link Parks, Neighborhoods in Baton Rouge," The *Times-Picayune*, March 5, 2013.

219 Diana Samuels. "Baton Rouge Mayor Officially Announces Government Street Will Undergo 'road Diet'" The *Times-Picayune*, March 19, 2014.

220 Tom Benning. "Dallas' New Bike Czar Is Ready to Roll; Her Thoughts on Hot-button Issues." *The Dallas Morning News*, July 19, 2014.

221 Christine Mattheis. "Worst Cities for Cycling: Where Cars Rule, Bike Lanes Don't Exist and Things Are Worse than in the '60s," *Bicycling*.

222 John Paul Shaffer. Livable Memphis. Webinar on FHWA's "A resident's guide for creating safer communities for walking and biking," by Pedestrian and Bicycle Information Center, February 10, 2015.

223 Eva Garcia and Ramiro Gonzales. City of Brownsville, Texas. Webinar on FHWA's "A resident's guide for creating safer communities for walking and biking," by Pedestrian and Bicycle Information Center, February 10, 2015.

224 Dug Begley. "Officials Hope Downtown Bike Lane Opens by End of Year," *The Houston Chronicle*, October 17, 2014.

225 Adriane Quinlan. "Where Cars Rule, Jefferson Parish Unveils a Plan to Encourage Bicyclists." *The Times-Picayune*, April 17, 2014.

Photo Credits

All images by the author except

Page 3   Diagram by Len Bahr

Page 20   Courtesy Yalla Let's Bike

Page 21   Clockwise from left, the photos are 1) Courtesy Yalla Let's Bike; 2) Courtesy Yalla Let's Bike; 3) by Kellen Gilbert; 4) Courtesy Yalla Let's Bike; 5) Courtesy Library of Congress

Page 46   Photo by Tricia Keffer

Page 90-91 Photo by Kirk Hunter

Page 117   Photo by Elly Blue

Page 120   Photo of "Unicorn Woman" by Tricia Keffer

Page 122   Photo of "Unicorn Woman" by Tricia Keffer

Page 123   Photos by Tricia Keffer

Page 125-127 Photo by Beaux Jones

Page 130-131 Photo by Donna Kennedy

Page 140-141 Photo by Beaux Jones

Page 146-147 Photo by Michael Boedigheimer

Photo 154 by Beaux Jones

Page 162-163 Photo by Elly Blue

Page 172-173 Photo by Elly Blue

Page 175   Photo by Stephanie Hepburn.